JOURNEY TO A DREAM

The First Portal

STEPHEN J. MCKOLAY

authorHOUSE®

AuthorHouse™
1663 Liberty Drive, Suite 200
Bloomington, IN 47403
www.authorhouse.com
Phone: 1-800-839-8640

First published by AuthorHouse 6/2/2008

ISBN: 978-1-4343-4245-4 (sc)

Printed in the United States of America
Bloomington, Indiana

This book is printed on acid-free paper.

For Ralph Thorpe

And

James McCormick

Friends and Editors

EDITOR'S NOTE:

To readers of all ages: Every now and again there is a book written that has something for everyone. This is one of those books. A story that tells a lot of great tales from when children could basically roam around freely and safely, and do things like play a game of football or baseball on a lot that was open and on which kids were allowed to play. The kids were well mannered, yet impish; trustworthy, yet inquisitive; and most of them were non-destructive and obedient to both parents and the law. Yes, these stories are fun, but underlying the whole story is the tale of a love that can only be described as "one-in-a-million."

This writer, Steve McKolay, has obviously led a soul-satisfying life and the story of his love for his wife and family brings with it a touch of the divine, (as in heavenly) and he leads all readers to remember things from their own lives. A fun-filled and extremely "give-us-a-good-inner glow" read.

Congratulations, Steve. You hit one of those home-runs you talked about in your recollections.

Ralph Thorpe

Stephen J. McKolay's narrative is a fascinating kaleidoscope of one man's life, full of anecdotes from boyhood which are so fully fleshed out that you, the reader, are left with a sense that the writer (and you) were there yesterday. The writing is poetic at times and philosophical now and then, but the heart of the book is the Tom Sawyer like adventures of a spunky kid of the Detroit of yesteryear.

The story, sub-plots and poetry are touching and smack of a pure heart. I, as a reader, was captivated by the goodness of the characters. The text is full of lots of nostalgia for older readers. Steve's vivid and philosophic memory makes for a good mental picture of events from so long ago. He has an unusually detailed memory of so many episodes from childhood which are recalled in a very believable way. The detail is very effective. This is real, "Tom Sawyer" stuff. Good story telling!

James R. McCormick

Author: Jerusalem and the Holy Land:

the First Ecumenical Pilgrim's Guide

ACKNOWLEDGMENTS

Throughout our lives we encounter many people and forces that shape our very existence, influencing how we conduct our lives. When I recollect on my own life, I realize that these individuals and events are far too numerous to list here in this text. It goes with out saying that all are remembered with great gratitude and respect. There are, however, a few that I wish to recognize. To my wife of 34 years, Celia, thank you for always being there and your enthusiastic encouragement you have provided throughout our marriage. To my parents, Stephen and Hedy McKolay, thank you. To my children and grand children, thank you for your support. I further wish to acknowledge all who have participated in this project, either real or fictional characters. As you read this text, there are mentioned many specific people that have had a profound influence on my character, please know that you are duly acknowledged. Thank you, God, for this wonderful life.

JOURNEY TO A DREAM
THE FIRST PORTAL

My name is Ewan. The narrative I am about to detail is on the subject of one man's life and how he lived it.

It was on a late day in September that I arrived at grandma's house. My mother asked me to assist in sorting through my grand parents' personal possessions that had been stowed away in the attic for many years. Mom instructed me to select a place and begin the process of sorting. Looking for a starting point, my eyes caught sight of an old black chest that rested in the corner of the attic. The chest had large gold latches and its corners were reinforced by gold braces.

I recalled seeing this chest before and remembered that as a child, I thought it to be a treasure chest. Grasping the center buckle I slowly opened the lid of this object of my childhood fascination. There, resting atop a mountain of old photos was something curious. I discovered a bundle wrapped in a white linen shroud. Removing the multiple wrappings of the shroud revealed a manuscript.

I called to my mother, who was rummaging through other boxes, telling her of my find. With her hand extended, she grasped it. On the cover, she read "Journey to a Dream". The author was none other than my grandfather, who passed on some two years earlier. Turning to the first page, she began reading. Then, unexpectedly she stopped, moved to the top of the stairs, and called to grandma.

"What is it Leigh Ann?, grandma said", "Mother, why is it that you never mentioned these writings by dad"? Grandma ascended the stairs and answered: "The book was a gift to me from your father. "Now is as good a time as ever to reveal it to you, your brothers, sister and my grand children". The three of us moved to an old leather couch that sat nearby. After a quick dusting, we sunk in to the old worn cushions and mom began to read the words my grandfather had written so long ago. When her eyes began to fill with tears, she paused, and turning to me, she said, "Ewan, would you please read from the text?" I extended my hand forward to receive the book. We were not aware that this chronicle had existed and were thrilled to discover what he had written. My Grandpa Steve had passed on some two years ago at the age of eighty-one. It began ....

JOURNEY TO A DREAM
THE FIRST PORTAL

With my eyes still closed and my mind wide-awake I acclaim, "Good morning, St Francis!" This was the first of the daily rituals I had become accustomed to each morning. Lying there, I sensed that for some reason this day would be extraordinary. Opening my eyes, I sensed a definite air of serenity and absolute relaxation that was absorbing my heart and soul. Lying there upon my bed I wondered, if today would be the day. Would the revelations I had received many years ago be coming to fruition?

Wiping the sleep from my eyes, I noticed that tears had moistened my fingers. The blurry sight of old age had vanished and somehow I was able to see clearly. I gazed at the ceiling and thought, what a miracle. My sight had been restored......was it just for the moment? I realized, in my heart, in this brief moment, that the answers to my questions were being confirmed for I recalled a wish I had made early in life. The dream I had sought was near at hand. Today, indeed, would be the day. It was as if I were reborn to youth. I recognized that my senses had regained their acuteness.

I looked to the left side of the bed to see Celia but she had already arisen and most likely was busy with her daily routine. There on the desk I noticed a calendar. It was displaying the date of September 28, 2032. The last date that I could recall was Christmas of 2022. So where had I been for the last ten years? In an instant, I viewed the past ten years of my life. I saw myself wandering aimlessly in utter confusion. It was revealed to me that I had been mentally asleep for a lengthy time, having succumbed to the devastation of old age disease, Alzheimer's.

Now, free from mental slumber, I knew that today the door would be opened. It was the fifty-ninth anniversary of my marriage to my wonderful, dear, wife, Celia. How strange, I thought, that I had not recalled our special day for many years, yet, today was unique. I looked to the top of my dresser where, many years earlier, I had deliberately positioned her photograph to see her smiling image, bidding me good morning. The clock to the left of her photo read 6:00 AM. I looked again to her photo and thought how lucky I have been to find such a life long companion as she.

This new day had begun and I acknowledged this reward and chose to make the most of it. I began this day just as I had begun each day of my life, with a few moments of prayer that included petitions to St. Francis and my guardian angel, Anthony, who I called Tony. I would ask them to safeguard and protect my family and myself this day. I prayed that through their intercession, when my time comes, I would experience a peaceful death, one of wonder and serenity. At that moment, in my mind I began to recite a poem.

THE COIN

Into My Hearts Treasury, I Slipped A Coin,

That Time Cannot Take Nor A Thief Purloin,

Oh Greater Than A Gold Crowned King,

Is The Safe Kept Memory Of A Loving Thing.

How extraordinary, I thought, that this Sara Teasdale poem which I had committed to memory some seventy years ago should once again enter my mind. Gazing upward my mind began to fill with reminiscences of time and events long since past. I felt like Rip Van Winkle rousing from a ten-year nap. I saw myself as a young boy attending St. Augustine School, standing in the presence of a Dominican Nun, Sister Rita Jerome. Visibly, I saw her teaching the class. She was explaining that our life's route is but a passage to a higher dwelling, and that what we achieve in our life prepares us for our ultimate reward. It also prepares and influences others who we will meet who are on their own journey.

She was a counselor who placed me under her wing, encouraging and reassuring me that everything would be all right. I came to understand that what she was saying was that our life is a test. How we live it is our testament. Academically, I faced many challenges, especially in the subjects of English, Reading and Math. Sr. Rita worked with me ceaselessly, and managed to see me through the first grade able to do my Math and improve my English and Reading skills.

Through her religious teaching, I became educated and came to understand that we are called by God to set a good example. She said, "Be strong in your faith, walk the walk and talk the talk. At all times, look for the good in people. In doing so you collect graces which are stored in your spiritual bank, available for withdrawal when, during your life you might need them." With her hand on my shoulder, looking truthfully into my eyes, she said, "Steve, you must seek out wisdom all the days of your life." I replied, "Sister what is wisdom?" She answered, "It is the gift of understanding that allows you to make good decisions as to how you conduct your life. As you mature it will come to you, if you search for it."

When my grandmother on my father's side died, I happened to overhear an exchange my dad was having with his sister, Aunt Maria. They were discussing grandma's passing. Aunt Maria said she had heard that when we die our lives flash before us in an instant. My father replied: " I believe this to be true". They were hoping this to be factual, for my grandmother's sake.

This conception had bothered me for a long time. At an early age I began to include in my many daily petitions to my spiritual guides a request, an expectation, that through their intercession, prior to my calling, I would be granted the gift of reviewing my life experiences in vivid detail. I trusted that my time here on Earth would be extended long enough to allow me to share the experiences of my life. I prayed that God would grant me enough time to recall many of the moments and events of my life, not in a flash while unconscious, but while living and breathing and in full consciousness. I intended to accumulate a wealth of spiritual graces during my life. I would place myself in good position, so that when my time came, I would be able to extract an enormous withdrawal from my spiritual bank account. I would cash in all my earned stipends. I hoped to be called from this life before my wife, my children and grand children. I requested a little extra time to record the joys of my life before the Pearly Gates would come into view.

My daily appeal ended with this final petition; "Lord, grant me the knowledge to accept the pain and misery of life, to see them as challenges, not persecutions, and grant me the wisdom to see that from all bad comes good. Give me the fortitude to seek contrition, and grant me forgiveness for all and any transgressions I have made." My faith in these matters was firm. I truly believed that God would grant my request if I stayed sincere to my pursuit.

Today was indeed a distinctive day. I could sense it. I looked up and smiled in anticipation of what this day would bring. I was fully aware of what the conclusion of the day would bring for me. Through a revelation, many years earlier, I was aware of what the events of this day would bring. Accompanying my state of relaxation was an impression of excitement. It was vividly apparent that He was granting my lifelong wishes. I accepted these premonitions for what they were, the answers to my prayers. I sensed that Tony was standing there beside me at my resting place. He is my constant companion. Together we recalled a composition of un-authored prose. I have placed it here for you, the reader, to ponder.

FOOTSTEPS

One night a man had a dream. He dreamed he was walking along the beach with the Lord. Across the sky flashed scenes from his life. For each scene, he noticed two sets of footprints in the sand: one belonging to him and the other to the Lord. When the last scene of his life flashed before him, he looked back at the footprints in the sand. He noticed that many times along the path of his life there was only one set of footprints. He also noticed that it happened at the very lowest and saddest times in his life. This really bothered him and he asked the Lord about it: "Lord, you said that once I decided to follow you, you'd walk with me all the way. But I have noticed that during the most troublesome times in my life, there is only one set of footprints. I don't understand why when I needed you most you would leave me." The Lord replied: "My son, my precious child, I love you and I would never leave you. During your times of trial and suffering, when you see only one set of footprints, it was then that I carried you."

With Tony's hand in mine, I accepted this gift, rose from my bed and began this last days' walk in full anticipation of the memories that would return. As I stood, I felt tears of joy stream down my cheeks to the side of my lips. They tasted sweet as they dripped to the side of my mouth. My frail legs, which for the past 10 years shuffled me gradually to my destinations, now carried me effortlessly, signaling that today I must hasten to my call. I recognized that I had received a spiritual cure that had renewed my body and soul.

I walked to the dresser and once again gazed at the photo of Celia. I picked up pen and paper and drafted a message of love to her, celebrating our anniversary. By the time I finished I had penned an essay full of prose and poetry. It started,...... To my dearest companion........... I placed the document atop the dresser for her to find later that day. I wanted this love letter, this gift, to come to her as a surprise. A surprise it would be, as it had been ten years since I recalled our anniversary. I showered, shaved and dressed myself effortlessly, then happily walked to the kitchen where I found her. I placed a tender kiss upon her lips and wished her Happy Anniversary. Her eyes at first displayed wonderment and then flooded with tears. She seemed contented and then embraced me, whispering her love and devotion in my ear. She immediately recognized that something was different about me today. She appeared perplexed and did not know if she should cry or laugh, be worried or happy. Then she asked me, "What's come over you today? How is this possible?" I briefly presented some elements of the epiphany I was experiencing so as not to alarm her, for I knew what the end of the day would bring. I told her that I believed that today would be a special day. I said: "Today I will set forth on a journey through my safe-kept memories and recall instances in my life that brought me to where I am today". It was story time. It was like looking through a box of old photos where every picture represented a thousand words. I could not help but be awe struck that this event was happening and especially on this day, my anniversary...there was no better day than today. I had sensed an impression of wonderment in Celia. She first seemed astonished at my recovery but then appeared prepared. It was as if she too, were waiting for this day to arrive.

I walked to the living room and sat in the old worn rocker and closed my eyes, not for my customary morning nap, but waiting for my anticipated recollections. Suddenly, I was under the driving influence of my father's spirit. He had long since passed away and memories of him began to flood my mind. What a noble man, I thought. I remember him telling me: "Steve, you're special, you're a dreamer and a philosopher."He gave my life direction and order. God, Family, Country and Job, in this order, was the path he taught. He challenged me to commit to memory the "7 Gifts" and the 12 Fruits" of the Holy Spirit. He said, "Steve, your life's journey will be guided and rewarded if you can value these qualities and always be conscious of them." I believed him, memorized them, and have ever since carried them in my heart. I have never forgotten the, "Gifts" of Wisdom, Understanding, Counsel, Fortitude, Knowledge, Piety and Fear of the Lord, along with, the "Fruits" of Charity, Joy, Peace, Patience, Kindness, Goodness, Generosity, Gentleness, Faithfulness, Modesty, Self-control and Chastity. Dad taught me loyalty, and that searching for truth and justice was a noble cause. The more I thought about it, the more I discovered that my character and attitudes were developed by the influence of these virtues as well as the influence of many significant people in my life including my wife, parents, family, friends and teachers. Implanted in me were these qualities. I sought to live my life by them and put them into practice in the day-to-day experiences of life. Some of them came early in life, while others came along later. I thank God for all my family and friends. It was appropriate that these thoughts came to me so early on this special day.

Turning my eyes to the left, I caught sight of the cherry wood wall clock as it chimed; it was 6:30 AM. The clock was a gift to my wife on our 22nd anniversary. Every quarter hour it chimed a portion of the "Ave Maria". At each hour, the full canto was heard. How lovely to be reminded of passing time this way. For me this day will be a celebration.

The rays of the sun began to cascade through the slots between the blinds of the bay window. The dawn of the day was calling. I arose to walk these last few miles. The end of the rainbow was in sight. I was convinced that the treasure I sought was at its end, for an exit was in sight. Opening the front door, I headed for the paper box to retrieve today's news. Celia loved to read the morning paper. The smell of autumn was in the air and the leaves of the trees began to transform the landscape into a work of art. A warm breeze seemed to make the trees dance before my eyes. I returned to the kitchen, placed the paper on the table and told Celia what a beautiful day was upon us. She turned and in her hand was a plated cheese omelet she had prepared for my breakfast. There is nothing better than a cheese omelet. Devouring it within minutes, I was satisfied. I asked her if she knew where I might find the photo albums we had amassed over the years. Her reply was that they are still in the cabinet where they have always been. I rose from the table, placed my dish in the sink and headed for the living room. I opened the cabinet and removed the photo albums. The next hour was spent leafing through them, viewing and recalling moments of happy times. Viewing these photographs was pleasant, for the majority of them mirrored delightful moments. I was content and smiling. I felt nostalgic and found myself thinking about my youth. It was then that I began to recall days spent with my grandfather. My mother's dad was an incredible man.

DAYS AT GRANDPA'S HOUSE

I derived a great deal of enjoyment when I was with my grandfather. He was born in Poland and immigrated to the United States in the early 1900's. His aptitudes and talents were many. He seemed to know everything about everything, so the saying goes. He had mastered all the areas of a skilled worker in many fields. He was determined to pass them on to me by giving me hands-on experiences. I spent many Saturdays with him. Dad would drop me off at his home early in the day. He treated me as his protégé and his apprentice. He had acquired a master's skill as a stonemason, carpenter, barber, plumber, electrician, shoemaker and gardener. He was passionate about his faith, the card game of pinochle and the standings of the Detroit Tigers. He never discarded anything that could possibly have an alternative use. He was a man of great ingenuity and creativity. He was determined to educate me by teaching me the art of a skilled worker. I was his aide and together we created wonderful, stone and glass embedded multi level grottos. He precisely constructed various casts that he filled with wet cement. It was my task as to depress small stones and bits of colored glass into the wet cement. He taught me how to calculate angles, lengths, and widths and the proper use of carpentry tools. I learned about the skills of electrical wiring and plumbing. We completed many projects in his wood work shop including book cases, bird houses, shelves and engraved address plaques. Grandpa provided me with hands on training, that I found to be quite enjoyable.

I have prided myself throughout my life at my ability to build or repair things around my own home.

Grandpa was a bit of a philosopher as well. While we worked on different projects, he would talk to me about his life and his beliefs. He told me that life is a series of decisions and choices.

In my vision I, see myself standing near the front door, fastening an address plaque to the wall. I had made this from scratch without any assistance. I took great pride in displaying it there on the front of my parent's home. There on the plaque was displayed the numbers of my boy hood home, 17241 Justine Street. I was standing on the sidewalk watching my brothers and sisters, mom and dad, busy with that day's activities. The next instant I saw them pass me in single file fashion, then vanish. To see all of us in our youth was an enjoyable encounter. With my hands still resting upon the top of the box of photos, I withdrew a snapshot of myself. It was a picture taken the morning of my first day of school, kindergarten. A twist of my wrist, my watch showed 7:00 AM. I then recounted this story.

STUCK IN THE "C" GROUP

Growing up in a large family was an occurrence shared by too few. By the time, I began school there were eight family members with another on the way. It was 1955 and my parents made the decision to enroll me in kindergarten at the age of four making me the youngest child in my class. I would not reach my fifth birthday until December 26, 1955. At that age, it did not matter to me because I had no idea what was to come. I felt right at home with my classmates as we all learned the basics of social interaction and became experts at clay molding and coloring. We learned the art of bladder control and the relief experienced when your teacher responded to your raised hand, politely excusing you to use the restroom. The whole class became proficient in poem recitals and choral presentations. Milk and cookies became the favorite pastime. The good nuns there at St. Augustine Catholic School, on the Eastside of Detroit, worked hard to imbed the golden rule in our hearts and minds. Like all schoolchildren of that age, you were proud of your accomplishments. To have my accomplishments acknowledged by my teacher, Sr. Mary Bernard, my classmates, and especially my parents was a wonderful thing. That first year came and went too quickly. The new friends you'd made suddenly had vanished leaving only the promise of summer vacation accompanied by the memories of the year gone past and the promise of the next school year, first grade.

My classmates were a year older than I was. My expectations were high and I welcomed the new school year with a great deal of enthusiasm.

My teacher was a sweet nun named, Sr. Rita Jerome. The boys in the class, including me, were infatuated with her because not only was she sweet in her nature but also she was a very beautiful woman. We had wondered how such a beautiful woman could choose the life of a nun.

Back in those early years of schooling, the class was divided into groups based upon your ability. First, there was the "A" group. This group was comprised of the most gifted of the class. You would have thought that some of the children in that group were walking dictionaries. Some of them were able to read "Dick and Jane" so quickly that, surely, they must have been tutored by Evelyn Wood herself. When it came to math, those in this group were the undisputed champions of addition and subtraction. There were two other groups. The second group was the

"B" group and the third was the "C" group. Membership to these two levels was determined by your success or failure in spelling bees, math bees and reading speed. If there were 24 children in the class, each group would have eight members. The weekly competitions would place you into the following week's designation. The theory was that if you worked very hard you could move yourself up to the next higher level.

It was not very long into the first grade that I began to realize that I was not mentally prepared to compete with these older children. In retrospect, I realize now that my parents had made a poor decision and started my formal education too soon. I was now in the first grade but having a kindergarten mentality. Around me, my classmates were excelling in reading, spelling and mathematics. I found that I struggled ever so hard to understand the concepts. Sr. Rita also realized that I was having a great deal of difficulty. I was convinced that it was impossible for me to rise to the next level and I; in fact, found it equally impossible to rise off the number eight position of the "C" group.

Day after day, I began to dread the thought of going to school. Just the thought that I might be called upon to read aloud sent shivers down my spine. I can recall a particular incident that had taken place. It was my worst nightmare. The teacher called upon me to read aloud to the entire class. My inability to read the words was so completely humiliating that I thought I was going to die. Sr. Rita tried to help me through the reading by announcing to me every other word that I, being choked up and on the verge of tears, repeated aloud through a voice low in volume. I will never know how I made it through that moment.

That specific incident goes down as one of the most terrifying instants of my life. For many years, I attributed my fear of public speaking to that single experience. My classmates were cruel and unrelenting. I became known as the boy who could not read, could not spell, and could not add or subtract.

Recalling this experience prompted me to smile. I seemed funny to me that I worried so much. It taught me patience and understanding.

I placed the photographs back in the cabinet, stood up and went back to my bedroom. My old catchall, desktop organizer/vanity was resting there atop the dresser. There was a larger drawer located on the bottom. It was in this drawer that I would place items that I believed might have some importance to me at a future date. Sliding the drawer open, I began to shuffle through all sorts of small objects that over the years had found this resting spot.

I placed my hand on a small pin. On it was inscribed the word "Page". This pin designated what I had achieved; it was the first level of ranking as an Altar Boy. As I looked toward the clock it was now 8:00 am. With the blink of the eye, I saw myself as an eight year old, sitting in my room trying futilely to memorize the Latin prayers of the Mass. I remembered thinking that it was critical that I master these prayers if I am to become an Altar boy. In the end, with hours of study and repetition, I did commit them to memory. I was accepted into the Alter Boys. Watching myself, recalling this struggle, a related memory entered my mind.

THE LITTLE ALTAR BOY

There were seventeen of us in the family, myself, six brothers, eight sisters and mom and dad. I was the third child and the eldest of the boys. When the size of my family was mentioned, the phrase, "You must be Catholic", was the usual query. I would reply, "Yes". As was mentioned earlier, my brothers, sisters, and I were enrolled at St. Augustine Catholic School located on the Eastside of Detroit Michigan. Our teachers were the Dominican Nuns, truly, Angles of Mercy. Many fond memories go back to those school days at St. Augustine. The Parish was huge and the church was an enormous Gothic structure. It still survives but is now a Baptist church because of the downsizing of the Diocese of Detroit.

When I was eight years old and in the fourth grade, I was recruited by Sister Rita Jerome to become an altar boy. My younger brother, Joe, had already been an altar boy for about six months. Most of my classmates were in the boy's choir or were altar boys, and I wanted to join the crowd. Back in those days, the Mass was said in Latin and I, not being gifted with good reading and memory skills, knew I would find it difficult to memorize and recite the Latin prayers that are recited during the Mass. Joe would practice the Latin with me. It seemed like a futile attempt to learn the verses, trying to prepare me to recite them from memory. We would act out the Mass at home in the upstairs bedroom where there was a large window-seat we utilized as an altar. Joe would yell down to mom, "Steve is hopeless", "He can't remember anything". After many weeks of practice with Joe and a very understanding nun, I managed to pass my recital and earned my Page Pin, (This was the first ranking within the Altar Boy organization). I was so proud of my accomplishment and was ready to serve.

Sister Rita Jerome scheduled me to serve the 6:00 AM Masses the following week with Joe as my co-server.

Upon arrival to the church, you would enter the Altar Boy wardrobe room where you chose your vestments, a black cassock and a white linen surplice. After dressing into our robes, we were required to light the candles throughout the church. My dad was seated in the front pew observing every move I made. To light the candles we used a six-foot long lance, which had a wick and a small extinguishing cup at one end. When the Mass had ended, dad, while chuckling, commented that I looked like Sir Lancelot the way I carried the rod with my arm fully extended. After lighting the candles, we filled the cruets with wine and water and a small pitcher with holy water used for the washing of the hands. All that remained was the priests' cue that mass was about to begin. I remember being very nervous but within a few minutes the butterflies vanished and I managed to make it through all the Latin, mumbling and lowering my head when I came to parts I continued to have difficulty with. I was able to continue this cover-up for a few weeks. The priest would say to me, "Steve, I can hardly hear you, could you please speak up". Eventually, it seems it took months; I was able to recite all the Latin without error.

During those first few months, the following event took place. Prior to mastering the Latin, Sister Rita Jerome announced to the class that she needed four altar boys to volunteer and serve a funeral mass that day at 11:00 AM. I raised my hand to be recognized. I was selected to serve along with three of my best friends, Frank Lenzion, Greg Tomacziewski and Enzo Venitell. After a moment, our teacher excused us from class and we then proceeded to the church to prepare for the service. I had not served a Funeral Mass before.

For some reason, that day, the four of us were in a goofy mood. We were hardly prepared to serve this solemn Requiem Mass. Frank was always cracking jokes and Greg and Enzo were both big teases. They knew that I had not yet mastered the Latin and would never let me forget it.

We located our vestments and dressed. Father O'Brien assigned our duties. My assignment was to carry one of the candles. The name of the function that I was assigned is called, an Acolyte or candle bearer. My duty was to carry a candle and process along the side of the priest, meet the casket at the entrance of the church where the priest gave a blessing and recited a few prayers. We then proceeded down the main isle of the church to the altar where the casket was centered for all the bereaved family and friends to behold. Greg served as the other Candle Acolyte, Frank carried the Holy Water and Enzo carried the incense burner. Because we were in such silly moods I tried not to look into the face of any of my friends for fear that I might start laughing.

When the mass began, we exited the Sacristy and made our way to the altar where Father O'Brien began to pray. You could hear weeping and sobbing in the church as family and friends of the deceased were overcome with sorrow.

The Mass was proceeding fine until the time came for Enzo and I to retrieve the cruets of wine and water. We climbed the four stairs to the top of the altar and presented the gifts to the priest. As I raised my foot to the last stair the toe of my shoe caught the cassock hem and ripped out a section about two feet long. Frank began to laugh and his reaction caused the rest of us to follow suit. Father signaled us to exit the altar and compose ourselves.

In the Sacristy, I asked the guys not to look at me while on the altar or I might start laughing all over again. I said, "Get your acts together, stop laughing and show some respect for the congregation." I quickly changed the torn cassock and within a few moments, we were back at the altar.

Within moments, Greg was unable to control himself and began to giggle once again. He grabbed his nose, covered his mouth, and made his way back into the Sacristy. Frank followed suit and lost control, so he likewise vacated the altar. Enzo and I did all we could to maintain our composure. We were at a point in the Mass, where the Altar Boys were to recite a Latin prayer, suddenly, everything went blank. I started to say the prayer, got through a few words then completely forgot the rest. I continued to mumble and speak gibberish hoping to cover up my embarrassment. Father turned and looked at me as though I was either nuts or speaking in tongues. Enzo heard the sounds I was making and began to laugh uncontrollably. He was snorting and laughing, his head bobbing up and down as he struggled to gain control. Finally, he had to remove himself from the altar as well.

From the altar, you could hear the laughter in the Sacristy as the three of them tried to overcome their folly. I kept thinking how awful this must be for the family and friends of the dead man to be witnessing such a display.

Father, very stoically, entered the Sacristy door, glanced at the guys and summoned them back to the altar. The remainder of the mass went fine and without a hitch. Father gave the most wonderful eulogy for the dead man. There was not a dry eye in the church and all of our shenanigans had been forgotten. Father must have felt that his prayers were answered; somehow, he thought, he and we, had made it through the service. He thought too soon! Read on!

The four of us felt remorseful about our behavior and we were deeply moved by Father's sermon. At this point, we certainly had angelic faces and any embarrassment we may have caused was forgiven.

We began our procession out of the church. Father was leading the way. Beside him were Greg and I, carrying our candles. Enzo with his incense and Frank with his Holy Water were directly behind us. The choir was singing a beautiful recessional hymn as we moved slowly toward the entrance of the church. A moment later, I heard a scream from the congregation. A woman shouted out that the altar boys' shirt was on fire. Sure enough, it was true. I had tilted the candle I was carrying and ignited the sleeve of my linen surplice. I had not noticed it. Instantly Father grabbed the Holy water from Frank and doused me. There I stood soaking wet. Father was overcome with embarrassment. Frank, Enzo and Greg were laughing so hard that the entire congregation began to laugh. Father had a stern look on his face. His expression was telling me unmistakably to exit the procession and return to the Sacristy. As I turned, a woman approached me. She was the spouse of the deceased. She asked me if I was ok and added that, I should not feel badly about what has happened. She commented, "My husband loved to laugh and would have wanted to go out this way. Why, he's probably responsible for all of this".

After mass, it was customary for the priest to give the altar boys a blessing in the Sacristy. As we approached him for his blessing he said, "Steve, you have already been blessed in fact you were baptized again and you three other guys, although you don't deserve it, kneel down and pray for Gods' blessing." He blessed us all in the Name of the Father, the Son and the Holy Spirit.

Now, here on my 81st birthday, I still wonder at this story. It is a testament and proof that Christ is always walking next to us. To think that an eight year old, a mere child, could experience all the many emotions, which were presented in that short one-hour Mass.............. I thought about this for a few moments longer and was grateful to have recalled the event. I turned to exit the bedroom and found myself standing in front of the full-length mirror that was fastened to the backside of the door. I looked at myself and smiled at the figure before me. "A Baby Boomer", born after World War II; look at me now!

With a song in my heart, I headed down stairs anticipating the next recollection, for I knew another was coming. On the kitchen table laid today's newspaper that I had retrieved earlier. The sports section was on top. The headline read, "Baseball Playoffs Near."As a youth, I loved baseball. Instantaneously, I could sense my father's presence. He was delivering the key to unlock another event. It was 8:30 AM.

MY BURIED TREASURE

Dad and I went shopping for a baseball glove. I was seven years old. After trying many models, he purchased a beautiful Wilson baseball mitt. It was the Al Kaline model. Al was my baseball hero. From the time that I was old enough to play ball, I dreamed of being a professional baseball player. I wanted to be like Al Kaline.

Al came to the majors around 1955. I would have been five years old then. He had won the Triple Crown and as far as I was concerned, he was the greatest ball player of all time. I cherished that mitt, taking it to Tiger Stadium with hopes of catching a fly ball or getting Al to autograph it. Quite often dad would take Joe, Grandpa and I to the ballpark.

After one of the games against the New York Yankees, we hurried down to the exit gate where the ball players would exit the park. A tall fence was the barrier that kept the fans isolated from their heroes. With my nose pressed up against the cyclone fence, Dad managed to spot Al as he came through the clubhouse door. He yelled Al's name, got his attention and asked if he would sign my glove. The security guard opened the pass through gate and allowed us to enter.

Al shook my hand then autographed my mitt. He and my dad exchanged a few comments as I glowingly looked up at my hero. I thought I was in heaven as I was in the presence of this young 6-foot tall super hero. Within moments there were 50 or more kids surrounding him asking for autographs or a chance to shake his hand.

I loved going to Tiger Stadium to see all the great players. I consider myself lucky to have seen such great players as Mickey Mantle, Roger Maris, Rocky Colavito, Charlie Maxwell, Jim Bunning, Norm Cash, Jim Northrup, Reggie Jackson, Whitey Ford, Harvey Keene and so many others. It was a major event each time I was able to attend a game at the ballpark. I lived for baseball. I guess you could consider me a baseball fanatic.

All summer my pals and I would play ball from sunrise to sunset. We would play right through lunch and dinnertime. It was easy to satisfy our appetites with a nickel Popsicle purchased from one of the many ice-cream vendors who rode their ice-cream bicycles around Jayne Field Park. Upon hearing the sound of their jingle bells, we would take a five-minute break from the game and enjoy one of these frozen treats.

All of the guys were good ball players. I was convinced that my ability came from my Al Kaline mitt and my Ken Boyer, Louisville Slugger bat. What a bat! It was thirty-two inches long with a large knob end and a very narrow handle. When I got hold of the ball, it soared. My reputation as the long ball hitter of the group was definitely a result of that bat. I must have hit a thousand home runs with it.

If we were not playing ball we would be watching it on TV or trading baseball cards. I spent any extra money I had on Popsicles and baseball cards, so it seemed. I would stop at the party store and buy those twenty-five cent packages of baseball cards. Wrapped in the package you found a stick of bubble gum and a few baseball cards.

Your eyes would fill with excitement and anticipation as you began to view the cards. I would scan the cards to see if I had been lucky enough to get any Detroit Tigers. I had a collection that was the envy of all my friends. I kept my cards very neatly sorted in a shoebox. The cards were filed by team name with each teams' super stars located on top. I had a second box where I kept all my doubles. I would trade and pitch cards from my doubles box.

Pitching cards was a great game. I would spend hours with my pals playing it. The rules to the game were simple. You and one, two, or more of the guys would pitch a card to a wall trying to get it as close as possible. The card closest to the wall won and would claim all the cards tossed that round. If you threw a leaner, you were a sure winner unless one of the other people had a leaner also. (When the card leaned against the wall). When two or more players threw leaners against the wall, the cards were equally divided between them. If your leaner covered someone else's leaner, you won. Every now and then, you would win cards, which could be added to your collection.

I used to spend hours looking at those cards and reading the statistics on the back. I knew all the vital statistics on most of the super stars of that era. As I grew out of this collection stage, the cards became less important and the entire shoebox collection just rested on the floor of my closet. The joy of that era was ending as I became occupied with other things and interests.

I had the brilliant idea that I should bury the collection, to preserve it for posterity. I was sharing that closet with four other boys and if I didn't do something to protect my collection, it would surely be destroyed. First, I needed a treasure chest. Yes! I decided that I would use my Davy Crocket metal lunch box. At this time, I was nine or ten years old and I did not use the old lunch box anymore. You know how kids are; I must have been in the fifth grade. If I had taken that lunch box to school, I surely would have been laughed at. The lunch box was perfect; it was metal and had a latch.

I placed all the valuable cards into plastic bags and then carefully inserted them into the box. I then taped the box shut and placed it into a plastic bag as well. I located the shovel and dug a hole at the rear of the house. The hole was about four feet deep and located about five feet from the house and four feet from an access door, that went under the back porch. I buried the treasure and felt secure knowing where it was. I was the only one who knew about it. My intentions were to return later and recover the treasure when I was older.

That winter, my parents announced to the family that we were moving. They had been looking for a new home and had come to a decision at that time. We moved from Detroit to the suburb of Westland. Being that the ground was frozen and snow covered, I was unable to retrieve the collection. I vowed to some day go back and unearth it. Year after year has passed and I have never returned to the old house to search for my treasure. The collection has most likely vanished from decay, but who knows, just maybe, just maybe I had dug down deep enough and wrapped it tight enough that it survived. It could still be there, intact and worth thousands and thousands of dollars.

I still have my Al Kaline mitt. I can see my boys, when they were teenagers playing with that mitt. The guys on their teams loved that glove and all of them, I am sure, got the same great feeling as I did when I placed it on my hand. I recall having the glove appraised back in the ninety's. At that time, it was worth at least one thousand dollars.

I walked to the closet, reached up, and standing on my tip toes, I felt the long forgotten mitt and brought it down. There was a package wrapped in a white shroud that was placed in the palm of my glove. I removed the package and placed it back on the shelf. I wanted only to feel my glove on my hand. I slid the fingers of my left hand inside, pounded my fist into the pocket recalling "Baseball".

For a few minutes, I reminisced, removed the glove from my hand and reached up to replace it back to its former resting spot. Something was in the way, preventing me from returning it to its former space. There, sandwiched to the rear of the shelf I found, of all things, a "Coon Skin Hat".

In 1973, Celia and I had purchased a replica of the hat, while on our honeymoon, in Gatlinburg, TN. We discovered it in a small gift shop. Placing the hat upon my head, once again I was transformed. I turned and caught the sight of myself in the full-length mirror that was fastened to the rear of the bedroom door. I looked and could not help but laugh. I thought, what a sight, an eighty-one year old man wearing a "Coon Skin," hat smiling at him self. I pictured myself holding, "Old Betsy", Davy's trusty long rifle. I raised my wrist to see the time. I noticed that it was now 9:30 AM.

BB'S AND WATER BALLOONS

As I walked from the bedroom, I recalled the Daisy Red Rider BB gun my parents had given me for my birthday. I had asked for this special gift, as I wanted to be just like Davy Crockett. I was about six years old at the time.

I was given very strict rules as to the use of this rifle. The only time I was allowed to use it was under the guidance of my dad. It was made crystal clear to me that I was not to go near the rifle unless he was present. He taught me the proper handling of the weapon. We spent many Saturday afternoons target practicing.

It was a hot late summer day, when, my friend, Tony, talked me into sneaking the Red Rider out of its secret hiding place. The rifle was concealed on the top shelf of my parent's closet. When the "coast was clear", I retrieved it. We moved to a tree covered lot a few hundred feet from my home and directly adjacent to Tony's house. I felt this to be a safe spot to target shoot. Our adventure would not be discovered as high brush and trees surrounded us. The burst of air from the gun could not be heard beyond where we were stationed. Tony and I must have shot hundreds of BB's at a paper plate that we used as our target.

An older neighbor boy, named Kenny, lived across the street. He had noticed us walking to the vacant lot concealing something. Kenny was fifteen years old. He surprised us as we were target practicing. He said, "does your dad know that you are using this gun?" I said, "no, please don't squeal on me". "If you let me try it, I won't say a word", was his reply. I handed him the Red Rider and he began to shoot at the target. He "Hogged" the gun and refused to take turns. He began kidding around by teasing Tony and I, saying, "I'm going to shoot you if you don't listen to me". Wanting to end this situation, I told him that I needed to put the gun back or I was going to be in severe trouble. He took the gun and crossed the street to his house, telling me he was going to play with it for a while. As I walked across the street to get it back, he fired at me hitting me in the hip. I fell to the ground in stinging pain and began crying. He was overcome with fear about his action and came running over to see if I was all right. I had a severe welt on my hip, fortunately, my blue jeans prevented penetration. Mr. Tomchek, our next-door neighbor witnessed the whole thing and reported the event to my parents. Kenny was punished by his parents and I, because of my disobedience lost the privilege of ever using my Daisy again. My mother was angry, as I heard her chastise my dad saying, "I told you that something like this would happen, I want that gun out of this house, now." Dad removed the gun from his closet, carried it to his car. He then drove to grandma's house where he stored it. It was never to be seen again.

I met up with Tony later that afternoon. As we walked down Nancy Street, we discussed what had happened. Tony told me he was sorry that he coerced me into disobeying my dad. I accepted his apology and we walked on putting the whole event behind us. As we walked, we had come upon a multi colored box that was lying on the sidewalk. Opening it up I found it contained ten individually wrapped balloons. We thought what a great find! Our plan was to return to my house, fill them up and have a water balloon fight. We opened the wrapper of a couple of them and attached them to the garden hose.

We were amazed at how they grew. I think it held a gallon of water and must have been three feet long. I took both of us to lift one off the ground.

Side by side, with the water in the balloon sloshing back and forth, we walked to show my mom the size of these great water balloons we had discovered. What a sight it must have been! When she saw us, she said, "Where did you get that?" I replied, "Mom, Tony and I found these giant water balloons down the street; Have you ever seen anything this big." She began to laugh so hard that we were perplexed. We thought, Why was she laughing? I asked her, "What's so funny?" She said, "Steve, those are not Water Balloons, they are used for medical purposes."I raised the box and began to read to her the letters on it, P R O P H Y L A C T I C. Mom took the package and said, "I have to return these to the hospital; they must have fallen off an ambulance."We thought, so much for our plan, another frustration. This made two disappointments in the same day. (It was years later that I came to realize the humor of the incident.)

Tony and I went upstairs to my bedroom where we discussed the events of the day. Except for the loss of Daisy, we agreed that it was in fact a good day. We placed the Ballad of Davy Crocket on my small record player singing each word from memory. Recalling this event, I saw myself singing, "Born on a mountain top in Tennessee", when yet, another recollection began to unfold. By my watch, it was 10:00 am.

Who was Davy Crockett Anyhow?

In 1955, I was five years old. It was at this time that Walt Disney Studios released a series of motion pictures that chronicled the life and legend of the legendary frontiersman, Davy Crockett. Little did he realize that these cinematic productions would capture the attention of an entire generation of children.

The series starred a new young actor named, Fess Parker. The characters', tall, good-looking appearance, captured the attention of the adult audience as well. The saga, which, Disney so masterfully brought to the screen (in color, I might add), would soon become a nation wide phenomenon.

In 1955, there were ten members of our family, mom, dad and eight children. My brother Joe was four. Joe and I were very close and were the best of friends. Mom and dad announced that they were taking the family to the theater to see, "Davy Crockett, King of the Wild Frontier". At this news, Joe and I were overcome with excitement and anticipation. Why, we just could not believe it. We were already the proud owners of a 45-RPM record that was titled, "The Davy Crockett Saga". It featured the theme song, "The Ballad of Davy Crockett" on the "A" side. As I remember, we just about wore it out as we played it repeatedly. We memorized the tune and the lyrics perfectly.

Dad whetted our excitement even more by the repeated promises of pop and popcorn. When the big moment came, I was completely lost in a fantasy world. From the beginning to the end of this ninety-three minute film, I was completely captivated, as was Joe. I can recall that, I just wanted to be just like Davy Crockett.

Disney portrayed Davy as a heroic figure. He possessed all of the wonderful virtues and attributes that any person could aspire too. Throughout the movie, you witness all of these qualities. All boys of the early fifties wanted to imitate him. We entered the theater as four and five year olds, but came out feeling like men. We learned about wisdom and love of family. We learned about love of country. We learned about understanding and perseverance.

When the show ended and we departed for home, Joe and I talked about going hunting, fishing and tracking. We practiced walking noiselessly through the woods and fields. How many times did I go to the mirror, in pursuit of perfecting the art of "Grinning Down", a Bear?

Learning right from wrong was probably one of the greatest attributes of the film. I viewed the story of Davy as a correlation of the King Arthur legend, just placed at a different moment in history.

This seemingly perfect man had a profound influence on the children of the fifties. Stand up for what is right and demand justice! Protect the values of your heritage and show respect for all people, even your enemy! The message it sent was to outwit your enemy, win the battle and then forgive the wrong!

At that time, the Motion Picture Industry did not permit moviemakers to display death in a battle. Valor and honor were the shields he wore.

You would not think it could get mush better than this but it did. The week after we viewed the movie, dad surprised Joe and I. He presenting us with our very own "Coon Skinned Hats" accompanied with replicas of the world famous "Betsy" long rifle. Mom offered buckskin outfits, fake rubber knives in leather pouches, leather-covered canteens and moccasins. Looking in the mirror, fully outfitted, there was now doubt that you had become the real Davy Crockett.

Walt Disney recognized the phenomenal marketing opportunities that came with this huge success. The

Disney Company as well as many toy-manufacturing companies inundated the country with every conceivable kind of Davy Crockett toy and memorabilia.

During that time of my life, I had fallen asleep many nights dressed in those buckskins with my trusty "Betsy", rifle at my side. The mania over Davy continued for many more months, as Disney released two additional full feature films. "Davy Crockett and the Riverboat Pirates", was the second release in the series. In this film, we learned the value of friendship. We understood that drinking and gambling were bad. The film portrayed that greed was indeed at the root of all evil. Ultimately you learned that there is good in all men and that like Davy, you have to sometimes search for it. The "Alamo", was the third film Disney released in the trilogy. In this film, we learned that, for justice sake, there will be times when we must make difficult decisions,Sometimes we are called to give up all that we have and live up to the character developed within us. Davy did just that.

He lived by his principles and decided to do battle for what he believed was right. His death at the Alamo goes down in history as one of the most valiant spiritual victories known. The cry, "Remember the Alamo" to this day, rest in the memory of many of us. This film taught us about the ultimate sacrifice, "To lay down your life for others". I found it interesting that the principles that governed Davy's life were those taught by Jesus Christ. In this legend he was portrayed as a true believer in the biblical teachings of Christ.

After pondering these thoughts for a while I looked once again to my watch, it was now 10:30 AM. Gazing at the side door I noticed a tower of black smoke billowing from my neighbor's chimney. Seeing this cascade of black billowing smoke evoked yet another recollection. I closed my eyes for an instant and upon opening them; I was standing aside a vacant lot in the neighborhood of my youth. I saw myself as a spectator, invisible to all there present. I was about to watch a magnificent sporting event..................

The Summer Football Game

It was a delightful morning, well into the dog days of summer. Dad was to take me to grandpa house for a haircut. I dreaded these haircut days. The clippers my grandfather used were operated by hand. Squeezing the handles together caused the blades to cut the hair most of the time. It was those times when the hair was not completely cut through that I dreaded most. These hairs would become caught in the blades and invariably be pulled from their roots. Ouch! More often than not he would unintentionally snag and pull the hair causing a great deal of discomfort. Each cut caused me to jerk and squirm. It was his opinion that I caused every mistake he made for not remaining motionless during the ordeal. While he was trimming my bangs, I jerked and moved resulting in a huge gouge of hair missing from my forehead. If my bangs had been teeth, it would have seemed that I had lost the two front ones.

It was now early afternoon. Dad and I returned home. My mother and my friends, after seeing me, found at my expense, far to much enjoyment from my appearance. After a few minutes of the usual ribbing and kidding the remarks subsided.

It was a scorching summer day and the guys and I found ourselves downright bored, yearning for some activity to occupy our time. At the age of ten or eleven, those long summer days have a tendency to be neverending. My friends and I gathered on the back porch to contemplate what we might do to entertain ourselves that day. The frustration of boredom was about to give birth to, "A Brain Storm". Brucie extorted, "Let's go and have a football game. Just because it is summer and we're right in the middle of baseball season, doesn't mean we can't play football." We all agreed and I and a few of my very best friends, including my brother Joe, Brucie, Waldo, Orest, Tony, Greg, Johnny and Ronnie jumped on our bikes and scoured the neighborhood rounding up as many of our buddies as we could find. We discovered that the idea was overwhelmingly accepted by all participants.

In the short space of about fifteen minutes, we all converged on the old sand lot located next to the cement manufacturing plant. The lot was the only vacant spot within the neighborhood that would accommodate our need of a playing field. This location was known to all as the "lot". We utilized this "lot" for activities from scavenger hunts to baseball games and the like. The cement manufacturing company owned the property and was kind enough to permit us to play there. We looked at is as a miniature city park and spent many hour there. Private property signs were posted around the lot, yet we were never asked to leave the premises.

This factory was a place where different types of cement, concrete and sands were manufactured, bagged and distributed to wholesalers. There was no access to the factory as it was surrounded and secured by an eight-foot high fence. It was obvious to all of us to stay out! The thirty-foot high building structure stood less than two feet from the fence. Looking upward, you saw two huge silos used for sifting sand that was first granulated then bleached and cleaned. We named this place, "White Sands". The finished product was sent down a conveyer where it was dispersed, creating a 30-foot high mountain of white sand. Located at the rear of the building was a smoke stack, which rose a hundred and fifty feet high. We had never observed any exhaust coming from it, most likely because our attentions were always focused closer to the ground.

When it came to choosing our teams, Orest and I being the eldest were always selected as team captains. Using the old odd/even finger draw, two out of three we selected our teammates. For those of you who don't know the method, you simply faced off and counted to three, whereupon you presented your hand either extending one or two fingers. You took turns calling out odd or even. If the sum of the fingers of the two captains was even and called out even, you won. The procedure was repeated until one captain had called correctly best two out of three. Whoever won has to choose first from the rest of our motley crew.

That day I won the draw and of course picked my brother Joe. He was the best athlete of our group and together, on the same team, we were unstoppable. We rarely ever lost at any athletic endeavor when we were on the same side.

Once the teams were decided, we proceeded to play ball. Viewing this from my minds vantage point, I recalled what a great game we played that day. Some of the plays we developed would have astounded the pros.

It was late in the game and the day was waning quickly for we had lost track of the time. A long time had passed since we heard the 5:00 PM siren blast that signaled the workers of the factory that their shift was completed. Orests' team had possession of the ball and was about to execute a play when suddenly the sky above became as black as the "Ace of Spades". The light of the early evening sun had disappeared. Orest called out "hike", upon which the ball was snapped to him. I noticed his course and

JOURNEY TO A DREAM

perusing him through the blackness, I tackled him. He and I abruptly arose from the ground saying what in the world is happening, as we could hardly see each other. One of the guys yelled out, "It's coming from the smoke stack, let's get the heck out of here. Hightailing off the lot, we ran a city block before we stopped, only to observe that from head to toe, soot covered us. We could hardly restrain ourselves from the humor in it all. Wiping the crud from my eyes, I looked at my pals, they looked at me, and we all burst into laughter. The sight was so hilarious that our laughter brought tears to our eyes. Our faces were painted with white streaks as the tears ran down our blackened cheeks.

From head to toe, we were completely covered with this layer of sticky, grainy soot that had emitted from the smoke stack. Who cared who won or lost the game? Joe and I retreated to home. My mother, upon seeing us asked, "What in the world happened to you guys?" She scarcely got the words out of her mouth, as her laughter prevented her from speaking. Immediately, we were immersed in the

58

tub where we scrubbed and scrubbed trying to remove the soot from our flesh. Mom was still laughing after we had bathed. While Joe and I were bathing, she had prepared two TV dinners. We carried them to the living room and proceeded to watch television, "Father Knows Best" was starting. I recall she laughed for many days thereafter.

Later we discovered that a worker at the plant had turned on an exhaust blower by accident while cleaning the furnace at the plant. It was now 11:30 AM. I began to recall the titles of many of my favorite TV shows of the fifties. Short snippets and excerpts of episodes flashed through my memories. Each morning while eating breakfast, we would watch Howdy Doody, Soupy Sales or Milky the Clown. In the vignettes of the Western serials I saw The Lone Ranger rear up atop his trusty white stallion, Silver. Roy Rogers and Dale Evans were vocalizing their Happy Trails ballad. Hop-a-long Cassidy and the Cisco Kid were at a full gallop upon there trusty steeds. I saw Cheyenne and Jim Bowie throwing their blades. Cheyenne's target was a far off tree while Jim

Bowie's was the front door of a log cabin. The Law Man and Matt Dillon from Gun Smoke were drawing their pistols in a gun battle against evil.

I spent my Saturday mornings watching these great shows of the fifties. The evening viewing brought us wonderful shows that embodied the philosophy of virtue and solid moral behavior. I see Lucy and Rickie, Ralph and Alice, Ed and Tricksie, Wally and Beaver. There, I see Donna Reed, Ward and June and of course The Father Knows Best show. We were entertained by the early game shows that included You Bet Your Life, Beat The Clock, To tell The Truth and many others. I could not help but think how an entire generation, known as, The Baby Boomers, were so profoundly influenced by this new media called the Television.

These thoughts were distracted when I heard Celia calling me, saying, your lunch is ready. She had fixed a tuna sandwich along with some Campbell's split pea soup. As a child, I recalled that this was one of my favorite lunches'. I recalled the old commercial, "mm, mm Good, mm, mm, Good, That's what Campbell's soup is, mm, mm, Good". I loved to immerse my sandwich in the soup adding additional flavor to every bite. From these thoughts, I found myself sitting in my parent's kitchen enjoying the same, identical meal. A few of my friends were invited to partake in lunch with Joe and me. While we ate, we developed plans to embark on an adventure. Joe, my friends, and I completed our pack and agreed to arrange our expedition and seek our quest. I recognized that another event of my past was being revealed when this event was disclosed.

GREEN HILLS

I and my fourteen brothers and sisters was raised on the Eastside of Detroit. There were seven boys and eight girls in all. We lived there from 1950 until 1964. Twelve of the children were born prior to our moving in 1964 and resided there. Our house was located on the corner of Justine and Nancy streets. Most of the people in the neighborhood were of Italian and Polish decent. In the city, an alleyway separated each block of houses. The alley was the route that the garbage collector traveled to gather up the rubbish. (We called him, "The Sheenie Man") This rubbish man was always a source of fascination because his collection vehicle was none other than a horse drawn wagon. To announce his arrival he would blow into a horn that made a sound that resembled that of a wounded bird. We all loved to see the horse as we seldom ever saw any farm animals in the city. I recall wishing that, "If only I could ride that horse, why, I'd be just like Roy Rogers and Hop-A-Long Cassidy".

When the Sheenie Man had made his presence known, most the kids would run to the fence just to see his horse. Mom would yell out," stay in the yard so you don't get run over or kicked by that horse."

Directly adjacent to our house was located an enormous factory. It must have covered six or seven square city blocks. As a child, I recalled how annoying it was to be awakened each morning by the sounds that came from of heavy equipment at work in the factory. Instead of hearing the sound of a rooster crowing, I was greeted by clanging and banging. Bumped up next to the factory there were about twenty rows of railroad tracks. Years ago, there once had been a city park located here. Many abandoned picnic tables, garbage cans and the skeletal frame of swing sets remained on the premises. Each row of tracks was offset by deep trenches, which were for water drainage. Dad told me how the Railroad Company and the factory had purchased this vast piece of the property, forever destroying this once fantastic place. He relayed many stories about the hours he had spent at that park before the factory and the railroad moved in. He went on to explain how the park had all the wonderful things you would expect. There were forested areas with hiking trails, fishing ponds, picnic grounds and playground areas. Within the confines of the park, there were two rows of towering wooded hills. These ran parallel to each other and were about a half-mile in length. Thus, the name, "GREEN HILLS", was adopted. What a great place! It was easy to imagine and envision how it must have been. He told us many captivating stories that, overwhelmingly, drove our curiosity. Quite often, he would reminisce about playing there. His great adventures just whetted our appetites the more. He told us of a swimming hole that was located in a secluded spot hidden deep within the valley formed by the two rows of hills. He vividly described how he and his pals would swing from a rope high up on the hill and soar above the pond, releasing their hold to make magnificent dives into the water below. He and his buddies had christened the place," BAB," a code that stood for, "Bare Ass Beach". They would swim stark naked, his reason being that he was too poor to have a bathing suit.

Joe and I were determined to see if any remnants of this place still existed. We made a pact that we would seek out this once marvelous place. Although we were forbidden to go near the factory, as it was an extremely hazardous place, we decided to find a way.

The factory was surrounded by a fence, which stood eight feet in height. This fence was topped with an additional one-foot barrier of barbwire. The fence seemed to be an insurmountable obstacle that we had to overcome. Peering through the fence you could see all kinds of heavy equipment and machinery. Trucks and pay-loaders were constantly moving back and forth, hauling all sorts of steel by-products, such as beams, pipes, and mountains of metal shavings. Occasionally we would encounter a person near the fence who would sternly warn us to keep out.

I was eight years old at this time and Joe was seven. We gathered some of our friends and told them of our planned adventure. Collectively, we agreed to proceed and bring our plan to fruition.

We were going to explore, "Green Hills" and search for BAB. We had designed a good plan with the help of Tony Cutsal. His house was kiddy-corner to ours and bordered the factory fence. The porch of his house came within two feet of the factory fence. Directly on the other side of the fence there was an abandoned house. The factory owned this house as it sat within their property line. It too was about two feet from the fence but on the opposite side. Both houses had raised front porches that stood five feet above the ground. They were enclosed by decorative rails, which were three feet above the deck. If you stood on Tony's porch rail, you were just a few inches below the barbwire at the top of the fence. The plan was brilliant and simple. After the factory closed for the day, about five o'clock, we would ascend to Tony's porch rail and leap four or so feet and land on the porch next-door. We were not sure what we might encounter once we got to the other side of the factory, but guessed we would most likely find another nine-foot fence. We made the decision to go forward, thus, our commando adventure began.

There was Joe and I, Bruce, Tony and Orest. The fateful moment had arrived and it was time to distinguish the professionals from the amateurs. The thought of making this long leap of faith from one porch to the other seemed easy enough, until I found myself standing on the rail, looking down and seeing that barbwire. I began to question myself, "What if I caught my foot on the wire?" I would kill myself I thought. We had a brief period of dares and double dares, chicken calling and so on. Finally, I decided I would do it. I bent my knees and leaped as high as I could, pushing forward. I actually landed better than five feet onto the porch. I found myself in no-mans land. The thought of it terrified me and I wanted company, so I encouraged the rest of the gang to make that same leap. One after one, they came across. All of us were proud of our fortitude and nerves of steel.

Gazing from the porch you could see parked trucks, pay-loaders, shanties and stockpiles of pallets. We feared detection by a security guard that might spot us and end our adventure. Like commandos, we moved from one place of concealment to another. After about ten minutes, we found ourselves at the fence on the opposite side of the factory grounds. Looking through the fence, we could see row after row of railroad tracks, just as my dad had said.

For a moment anxiety set in and my returning apprehension made me wonder, what would my dad do to me if I was caught? That thought lasted only a moment as I was now catching site in the distance of Green Hills, the object of my quest. The hills towered high on the horizon above the tops of freight cars that were stored in the railroad stockyard.

Everything was just as dad had said. Luck was with us as one of the guys, (I do not remember who), located an unlocked gate in the fence. We proceeded through the gate and began to make our way crossing one row of tracks after another, crawling under freight cars and leaping over the drainage ditches that were full of water. The ditches were just wide enough so that when you jumped your landing foot was soaked. These canals were full of frogs and pollywogs (tadpoles). We stopped for a few minutes and tried to catch some frogs; it was like being near a country stream. " Let's get going, we need to get over these tracks", I said. We moved on and made it past the tracks.

Now the hills were dominating our view. Wow! This is great! Let's go! We ran as fast as we could toward the hills. Temporarily exhausted from our sprint we were at the foot of the hills. Looking around we discovered a few old picnic tables and trashcans. They were all marked as the property of the City of Detroit, Parks and Recreation. It was just as my dad had described it, it was all-true. What about "BAB"? I urged our gang on, telling them that we had to find it.

We had come upon an old path, which led to the top of the hill. Once we reached to top, we could see for miles. Our house and neighborhood was not visible because the lay of the land and the distance we had come had placed them below our horizon. I thought about how my dad had been here when he was my age, perhaps this very spot. I was more determined that ever to find BAB. A narrow pathway along the top of the hill, led from one end of the hill to the other. Across from where we stood, you could see the other hill of equal height. It was about 75 yards to the other side of the valley formed by this natural upheaval. Somewhere down there was a pond. We figured that all we had to do was hike the entire span of the hill, looking carefully until we spotted the pond. After walking a short distance, one of the guys shouted out, "The Pond". Side by side and elbow to elbow, we gazed down in wonder to see this clear pond. It looked as though the bottom of the pond was layered with white sand. Our gang descended, undressed and went swimming. I was reliving the same experience that my father had when he was a boy. A knotted loop tied to a cantilevered bow on a huge oak tree was the only remnant remaining of the rope he had described in his account of BAB. An old toppled maple tree had collapsed and was resting with its two-foot wide trunk hovering a few feet above the pond. It served as a natural diving platform. It was as if we had found Shangri-La in this hidden valley of sure delight. When we had had our fill of swimming, we sat at the shoreline and ate our snacks of peanut butter and jelly sandwiches and pretzels.

We had embarked on this venture with the determined goal to be successful in our quest and we were victorious.

It was time to return home for we had been gone for three or four hours. We realized that our families were probably looking for us. The trek home was surprisingly easy for we knew the path to take. We knew the route to take, enabling us to avoid detection by the workers in the factory. We were great explorers who had conquered all obstacles that had come before us. We had returned the same way we had come by retracing our exact route. With our final leaps over the fence on to Tony's porch, our venture was completed. Mom had been looking for us, but we were careful not to be detected. We explained that we had been playing at Tony's house and she immediately accepted the statement, which was, in fact, partially true.

I wanted so much to tell my dad what we had seen, but was apprehensive to do so because I had broken the rules. It was not until a couple years later that he found out about it. The journey was made many times and many happy hours were spent at," Green Hills "and "BAB",(until we were caught by the Railroad Dick's). However, that is another story.

After reliving this experience, I sat there thinking how much fun I had as a child. Growing up in the city we, myself and friends had to be creative to entertain ourselves. Television was being introduced to the market place and my family was fortunate enough to acquire a set that had a round, eight-inch black and white screen. (Color TV had not been introduced at this time.) The screen sat within a rather large cabinet, standing about four feet above the floor. I recall dad telling all of us that today we would be watching a great movie. The title of this movie was, "Tarzan the Ape Man". After we viewed this great classic movie, my friends and I decided to create our own jungle. It was now 1:00 PM. I had had a great lunch an hour ago and relived, "Green Hills", so I was content. I peered out the slider door from the kitchen and noticed the old tree house I had built for my children back in the eighties. It now rested on the ground, far from the glory it once had when it rested high above the forest floor. Closing my eyes for a moment the next recollection was upon me.

BOOBY TRAPPED JUNGLE WALK

The entire family gathered around the television set to watch, "Tarzan the Ape Man". The featured stars of the movie were, Johnny Weissmuller and Maureen O'Sullivan. In the visualization I see, myself, my parents and eight of my siblings gathered around this eight-inch miracle television watching this great adventure movie.

As you may recall, our television was one of those early fifties models. The screen was eight inches round and the picture was in black and white. I was an early arrival to the event and managed to acquire a vacant seating place on the couch in clear view of the picture tube. It was like being a contestant in an intense game of musical chairs, too many bodies and not enough places.

After the seating spots in the chairs and couch were occupied the remainder of the family found suitable spaces on the living room floor. Dad had created so much hype and anticipation that we were all biting our nails, waiting for the show to begin. My older sister, Marcia, made popcorn and Mom put about a dozen TV dinners in the oven. (My favorite was the corned beef hash). There we gathered, with TV dinners in hand, waiting for the movie to begin.

It was a great event, what a movie! I will never forget how Tarzan fearlessly descended into the Gorilla pit to rescue Jane. With his notable cry, he summoned the elephants to his aid and vanquished the pagan tribe living within the Pigmy Village. The movie was a panorama of how good prevails over evil. The excitement of the moment was shared by all there present; it was a time, which would not be soon forgotten.

The next morning when we awoke, our conversation focused on this absorbing movie. During breakfast, my elder sisters, Marcia or Ramona, suggested that we create our own jungle, full of hazards and danger. They envisioned creating a pathway, which would lead you through many frightening encounters. We agreed to a fee of a nickel, for admittance to our exhibit. What a moneymaking enterprise! We were elated at the prospect of earning a lot of money. To augment those earnings we would sell Kool-Aid and cookies at a refreshment stand.

Who would have the nerve to venture through what we called, "The Booby Trapped Jungle Walk"? This was real Tom Sawyer or Little Rascals stuff. We had the idea and the motivation, the next thing was to find the location.

Being in the inner city, a wooded area to create this landscape was scarce at best. I suggested, "There's a densely treed lot down on the corner of Ryan and Nancy Roads"! It was about nine city blocks from our immediate neighborhood. All agreed that this location would serve us well in our endeavor. Our imaginations were running wild. We all participated in coming up with a variety of booby trap ideas. Collectively, we searched throughout the house, under the porches, anywhere and everywhere, searching for any item, that could be utilized to enhance the terror that we hoped to create. Rope, hoses, boards, flashlights, anything that might work, was tossed into a couple of wagons. My sisters, Joe, and I enlisted a few of our closest friend to help with creating the Jungle Walk.

Upon arrival at the site, I remember thinking, "This is a great place"! There were tall trees, huge shrubs and bushes. It appeared to us that we had just walked into deepest, darkest, Africa. The bushes were tall enough so that you could not see above them. All of our creative juices began to flow and by the end of the day we had transformed the lot and completed our work. We spread the word throughout the neighborhood that tomorrow; our Jungle Walk would be open for business.

We had cut a narrow maze through the woods with many turns and obstacles. The entrance was located in the alleyway. I had built an arched opening from branches and vines. Above the arch, I placed a sign that read, "Enter at your own risk, five cents, Kool-aid and cookies five cents." I had cut a medium size tree about two thirds of the way through, tide a rope near the top so as to keep it upright. At the precise moment, I would release the rope from my concealed position. This hazard created an effect that a tree was falling right on top of you. It worked great. One of my sisters was stationed inside a large pit we had dug. The opening of this pit was covered with boards and camouflaged with sticks and leaves. A small opening gave her enough room to extend her hand to grab the ankle of the person who passed. The next hazard encountered by our paying guests was a "trail trap". We excavated a hole three feet deep and filed the bottom with mud. This opening, too, was covered with thin branches, leaves and brush. I named it, "The Pit of Scum". Upon contact, the hikers would find themselves mired deep in the hole, covered in mud. Next on the journey, you would encounter a snare I had fashioned from a thin flexible tree. I did not manage to catch anyone; however, the startling effect of the snap of the snare was most effective.

We created many other special effects along the pathway. There was a simulated native campsite complete with a hut and campfire pit. We concealed one of my brothers behind the hut, where he created different sounds and noises to distract the passerby. He had tied ropes to nearby bushes and trees. Pulling on the ropes caused them to sway and rustle. This created the illusion that fierce savages and animals surrounded you. My brother, Joe, was camouflaged and stationed high up in a tree. His assignment was to drop acorns on top the head of the passerby. The trail exited near Ryan Rd. You could sense the relief of the kids as they once again saw the light of day as they exited the forest.

By the end of the day, so many kids had gone through the Jungle Walk that we had made over five bucks.

The next day we returned to clean up and remove the items we had used. On our way back home we stopped at Chinieski's (The local Candy Store), to spend our hard earned money. All had a great time. It was now 2:00 PM and I smiled to myself feeling delighted that I had remembered the event. With the blink of an eye, I suddenly found that I was hearing what sounded like a freight train. The rhythmic sounds of the wheels crossing seams in tracks were unmistakable. I looked to the sky and had a glimpse of an old Norman Rockwell painting flash through my memory.

THE KEYSTONE BUM

About eight city blocks from my house there was a city park named, "Keystone Park". The park was about twenty acres in size and was L shaped and completely enclosed by an eight-foot high cyclone fence. The railroad depot bordered one side of the park. The location was central to the moving of freight in the city of Detroit. Converging at this point was a network of forty to fifty track lines. At any time, you would see hundreds of boxcars on various tracks waiting to be loaded, unloaded and routed. It was common to see up to a hundred cars coupled. As the lead engine began to pull forward, the rhythmic movement of the cars was likened to that of a row of Dominos falling in succession. Accompanying this you heard the musical sound of each car as the forward motion locked the car couplers as the iron wheels began to move. The combination of the clicks bangs and squeals emanated a methodic beat and a song, which by some means produced a soothing tone. It was easy to calculate the number of cars in the line by counting the bangs that resounded in progression. It was easy to identify the many manually operated switches by their flashing green and red lamps. I would observe railroad workers operating these switches, routing trains throughout the interchange to unknown destinations. This scene was never ending. The constant repetition and the passage of time eventually made the sounds unnoticeable. The sounds became "white" noise, barely noticeable.

Back in the 1950's, the railroad was used as the primary methods of transportation of freight. I found myself looking at the cars as they passed to see where they had come from and often wondered what their final destination was. On the side of the cars was displayed the names of the different cities of their origin. Most common were Chicago, Detroit, Gary, New York and Los Angles.

Along the cyclone fence were posted "Keep Out and No-Trespassing" signs. These signs were ominous reminders of the danger that was present in the complex. The complex was patrolled constantly by security guards who's job it was to stroll the premises and checking each boxcar for stow away occupants who might be trying to conceal their presence. My parents warned, repeatedly, "Stay clear of the Railroad Yard". I recall my dad telling of an incident that took place near Mound Rd. A train had struck a woman while she was crossing the tracks. He vividly described that all that was left of her was bits and pieces. I never did discover if the story was fact or fiction but the account got the point across, "Keep Out."

One Saturday afternoon dad announced that the family would go downtown to take in a matinee movie at the United Artist Theater. The name of the movie was "Picnic". It starred William Holden and Kim Novak. I remember it. In the movie, William Holden traveled from place to place by stowing away in boxcars. The movie depicted him jumping on and off moving freight cars as they rolled from town to town. Dad made the comment that William Holden's character was that of a "Railroad Bum" and that I must be leery of such people whenever I was in the vicinity of the railroad yard. I remember feeling sorry for the character Holden portrayed in the movie. I recalled another movie production that was released some fifty years later. The title was "Dennis the Menace". One of the lead actors, Christopher LLoyd, portrayed a completely different type of "Railroad Bum", a sleazy criminal type. Lloyd's portrayed character was the type of bum that dad had warned me about.

My friends and I spent many days at Keystone Park. The city attendants to the park always had special activities planned. There was always something to do from baseball and football games, scavenger hunts, volleyball, basketball, shuffleboard, picnic's and barbecues, relay races, story telling, campfires, weenie and marshmallow roasts and the like.

One summer morning my pals and I met at the park for a day of baseball. There were enough gathered to staff two teams. We started playing ball early in the morning and ended late in the afternoon completing five or six games. The baseball diamond was located along the side of the park that bordered the railroad yard. We took turns shagging foul balls, that crossed over the fence, landing in the railroad yard. At times, a worker might be present and retrieve the ball for us. Usually it was up to me to quickly scale the fence and evacuate the ball without being noticed. I felt like a hero when I made my way back over the fence with the ball in hand. The other guys looked up to me because I was brave enough to take the risk of being detected.

As we played ball that day, one of the guys noticed a man sitting on the ground resting against a tree within the railroad yard. He was smoking a cigarette and watching us play ball. From where I stood, he appeared to be a tall, lanky and under fed man. I remember feeling sorry for him. He was obviously not a worker because of the way he was dressed. In my mind, I immediately deduced he was one of the bum's I had been warned to avoid. He looked rather harmless, especially knowing that the fence stood as a barrier from him.

If you have ever seen Norman Rockwell's portrait of a tramp you would have thought that this person must have posed for him. He wore an old plaid sport coat, which covered a light colored soiled shirt. His pants were old and faded blue jeans. He sported a small leather cap and his rough looking face was dirty and unshaven. You could see his socks protruding through holes on the soles of his once fine pair of shoes. On the ground next to him was a sack made from a red print scarf, which was fastened to a stick about three feet long. The sack probably contained all of his worldly possessions. He sat there for hours smoking one cigarette after another watching us play ball, minding his own business.

It was getting late in the afternoon and the railroad detectives, (Dicks as we called them), were making their rounds checking boxcars for stowaways. Their arrival was unnoticed by the tramp as his attention was on the baseball game. The railroad Dicks carried clubs. They would work in pairs as they checked each car. The two of them, on opposite sides of the boxcars, would slide open the doors and inspect the contents. You knew when these inspections were taking place by the rhythmic slamming of the doors as they were opened and closed. They would move from car to car.

Suddenly we heard someone yell out, "get that guy". The bum was as startled as we were. He immediately sprang to his feet, looked around and saw two big burly Dicks in hot pursuit of him. He immediately sprang to his feet. I noticed that he was a tall man, over six feet, and as skinny as a rail. The bum grabbed his sack and began to sprint along the side of the first line of track. His only escape was to out run the Dicks. We all watched at the ease with which he was able to elude his captors. He was able to tuck and roll under cars, hurdle the connecting clamps between the cars and leap the drainage ditches that separated each line of track. There was no obstacle to slow him down. It was like watching a graceful track star run an Olympic obstacle coarse. Within a few moments he had succeeded in evading capture.

He was a magician in the way he used the cars and ditches to conceal himself from the view of the Dicks. From my vantage point, I could see where he had taken refuge. He was about seven or eight track rows over from where he began and the Dicks were not even close to finding him.

As he was resting, the Dicks came over to the fence where we were watching the event unfold. They asked," Did any of you kids see where that bum went"? One of the guys yelled out, "Yeah, he's over in the ditch that way". Instantly the bum sprang from the ditch and began a full out sprint running in a mad dash to exit the railroad yard. His escape was about a half-a-mile away where the tracks crossed Ryan Rd. With his adrenalin surly pumping, that bum ran faster than any person I had ever seen.

A few minutes later the Dicks returned empty handed and told us that the "Railroad Bum" had gotten away. They lectured for a minute warning us of such characters and then went back to checking boxcar after boxcar.

Personally, I was happy that the bum had escaped. I later thought about him with sympathy feeling that he had been dealt a bad hand. I hoped, for his sake, that his life would get better. I rationalized that his escape was due to his superior speed and cunning. In my mind, I wished him well.

As this recollection ended I found myself again in real time. I was effortlessly walking outdoors to visit the area where our dogs, Velvet and Bonnie used to reside. They were both great pets. The fragments of the old doghouse I had built along with the hundred foot long cable spanned for their run were visible. I opened the door to the shed that was located next to the doghouse to investigate what contents it had. Old bikes, paint cans, scraps of wood and the like were found. I looked down after hearing a sound to find a red squirrel looking up at me. He had gnawed a hole through the floor and had taken up residence in the shed. I was intruding on his territory. The sight of him threw me back to recall a story about another furry little creature from the past. Seeing a lawn chair not far from the shed, I sat down to feel the breeze in my face, looked at my watch, it was now 3:00 PM.

RAT HUNTING

The house in which I resided was built years before the factory had acquired the city owned land to the North of the neighborhood. I can only imagine, but it must have been quite a beautiful site. All I ever had seen was this 8-foot high cyclone fence, which ran for eight or nine city blocks. The factory was just outside our door. As you would expect, the factory was an ideal breeding spot for rats. In all fairness to the factory, the pest control was really quite good. On occasion, you might catch a glimpse of a rat that had ventured out of the factory grounds into the neighborhood.

One day, my mother had the startle of her life. She had been in the basement doing laundry when one of these big city rats had darted across the floor and then behind the laundry area. This unfortunate critter had gained entrance into the house from an opening in the block wall. My grandfather was plumbing in a new bathroom and to route the plumbing he had removed a block in the foundation.

That day when my father returned from work, mom had relayed the incident to him and he immediately called Joe and I and informed us that we were about to go on a rat hunt. I was about 8 years old and Joe was seven. Dad was the kind of person who found security in numbers when it came to things like this. He sweetened the deal by telling us that when the job was complete, we would be awarded with a puff of his cigarette and swig of his beer. At the time, he was the chief safety engineer at the Ford Motor Tractor Plant in Highland Park, Michigan.

He announced, "Come on boys, we're going to find and eliminate that rat."

After hearing the conversation mom and dad had, you would have thought we were going on a wild game hunt. "Why, it was the size of a cat, mom said."

The basement was poorly lighted and cluttered with all kinds of stuff as you can imagine, having a household of 10 people. It was laundry room, tool shop, and storage bin and furnace room all in one. It was like walking through a maze of multiple garage sales.

That rat could be anywhere, I thought. I remember thinking that this monstrous beast might attack and inflict a mortal wound. We were embarking on a venture that had my hair standing on edge. Joe and I were frightened about the whole thing and really did not want to participate. Dad uttered a few words of wisdom as I recall, things like, "Be a Man", or, "Expect the unexpected". Descending into the bottomless pit (the basement), the adrenal juices were flowing like a raging river. Dad had a plan. He armed

Joe and me with brooms and himself with a hammer. We figured he was going to club the thing to death.

The plan was to start at one corner of the room and move everything away from the wall to flush out the beast. Joe was lucky because he had been stationed at the corner near the bottom of the steps. If he needed to escape an attack, his route up the stairs was right in front of him. I was stationed ahead of my dad who was moving things away from the walls. I was to beat the rat if it was successfully flushed it out. I did not relish my posted position. I understood it had to be this way. I was too young and physically incapable of moving the heavy furniture, boxes and appliances. With each item, he moved, I was prepared to slam the beast should it show itself. Dad would say, "Be ready Steve, it might jump out at any moment." He said to Joe, "Joey, be ready in case it back tracks, yell out if you see anything move." We all proceeded to stalk the creature.

It took forever to make our way around the perimeter of the room. Each moment that passed brought us closer to that eventual end. When we had reached the last ten feet of wall, we were all certain that the decisive moment had arrived. Gripping my broom tightly I waited as dad moved this huge old dining table. The rat had to be hiding there, I thought. What is this? No rat, dad exclaimed! I was relieved. The rat must have vacated the basement back through the opening. Dad had found some screen and decided to plug the hole until grandpa finished his plumbing. As dad had promised we were each given one puff of his cigarette (we were not allowed to inhale, in fact we did not even know how to) and one sip of his beer. We were very macho men.

While we sat at the bottom of the staircase savoring our puff and swig, there was a brief moment of silence, dad said," Quiet boys, I just heard something." We were so quiet you could have heard a pin drop. The silence was suddenly broken; first, we heard scratching followed by what sounded like the pitter-patter of little running feet. Slowly we moved to the location of the sound. It was coming from the ceiling above the tiles. Looking at each other, in unison, we yelled," The Rat."

That critter had found its way into the ceiling. Now all the anxious feelings had returned. The ceiling tiles were old and loose so dad decided to tear the whole thing down. Dad quickly went upstairs to gather up three pairs of safety glasses to protect our eyes. Being a safety engineer, he had a supply of them available. Armed with our brooms and he with his hammer we proceeded to remove the tiles one by one from the outside perimeter moving toward the inside. Each tile removal made the concealed area smaller and smaller. We could hear that rat scurrying here and there as it was showing signs of desperation.

Eventually there were only two tiles remaining. Dad positioned a ladder, had me climb up, and with the claw of the hammer yank down one of the remaining tiles. He positioned himself to slam the beast. I pulled and the tile came crashing down from the ceiling. No rat yet! He moved the ladder once again and instructed me to pull down the last tile. Here it comes! "Get ready dad", I said. With one final tug, the tile loosened and out leaped this monstrous rat. Leaping much further than my dad had calculated. He swiped his hammer catching the beast, as it was airborne. The rat being stunned and injured wiggled on the floor barely making any forward progress. Dad put it out of its misery with one sharp blow from a broom handle.

I was amazed at the size of the rodent. Mom had not exaggerated the size.

We were relieved that the hunt was over and dad surprised us again with one more puff and one more swig. The basement was a disaster zone. Tiles and fragment of tile were scattered everywhere. It took a few more hours to clean up the mess we had made. I could tell dad was proud of his accomplishment and I expected mom to shower her hero with all kinds of accolades. His success had him beaming as we ascended from the pit. He announced to all that we had done it! Her response once she saw the basement was, "Why didn't you just call an exterminator. Poor dad, no glory or honor for the unsung hero! We made numerous trips from the basement to the alley where we deposited enormous amounts of tattered ceiling tiles. It seemed like it took forever to clean out the basement. On the last trip to the refuse pile, I noticed that the "Sheenie Man" was approaching our home. He and his horse drawn wagon were in sight a quarter mile down the alleyway. It was now 4:00 PM.

THE SHEENIE MAN

As I mentioned earlier, in the city, between each block, there was an alleyway. The surface was gravel and about twenty feet wide. The alleys were there for ease of trash collection and maintenance on utilities. All the residents had their yards fenced about four feet high right up to the alley. We had built a rack, which supported three garbage cans. This rack was located against the fence and rose about a foot off the ground. When the garbage collectors came by it was easy to grab the cans, empty them and then return them back to the rack. If you looked down the alley, you would see that each residence had done the same.

Prior to collection day, the "Sheenie Man" always paid us a visit. I am not sure, but I think that "Sheenie" was Polish for "Junk". I deduced this because I remember my grandfather calling that name from my earliest childhood. Grandpa was Polish and he and my grandmother spoke the language often.

Early each Wednesday morning you would be alerted to his arrival. In the distance could be heard a blaring sound of a small mouth blown horn. It sounded like a wounded bird. What was unique about the Sheenie Man was that he still used a horse drawn wagon. We were always excited to see him. He was a raggedy old person, rough looking and dirty. His face was never clean-shaven and his clothing was old and tattered. Atop his head, he sported a small cap with a short bill. He wore it slightly cocked to the side and pulled down over one eye. He wore huge high-top leather boots that had not seen a polish brush in years. His pants were a light brown, stain covered; remnant of what was once part of an expensive suit. Over his torn and tattered, soiled gray T-shirt, he wore a weathered, plaid sport coat. When he smiled, he showed a beautiful set of pearly white teeth. He was quite the sight to behold. He sat high above the ground on a wooden bench which was secured to the old buckboard wagon. The wagon looked just like something out of the old west. The only thing missing was the canvas cover.

I kept imagining how neat it must have been to travel west in a covered wagon. I thought, boy, this old guy has it all: a horse, a wagon and all that good stuff loaded on it. Keep in mind that at this time and at my age, 5 or 6, we were in the era of Western TV shows, "The Age of Roy Rogers and The Lone Ranger." All the kids my age watched all the TV westerns, had our holsters and guns, cowboy hats, spurs and the like. To see a horse and wagon in the city was exciting. I always thought that Sheenie Man would have looked great if only he had a nice cowboy hat instead of that cap.

The Sheenie Man's business was kind of like a mobile garage sale. As he blew his horn, neighbors would rush out to pawn off all sorts of things, items that would not be collected by the city collector. He was a friendly man, always willing to stop and talk to us children. Can you imagine the stories he could tell? If you can picture his wagon, you would see used furniture, clothing, toys and hundred of things he must have believed had some usefulness. It was all free. He was the ultimate junk man, ahead of his time, a mobile flee market and resale shop. As he would," fade into the sunset", to coin a phrase, I still remember yelling out, "What's the horse's name? What is the horse's name?

It was now 5:00 PM. I had been sitting there in this chair for some time now. I arose and walked to the front of the house where I notice a young couple slowly walking past the house. They were pushing one of those double strollers carrying two infants. They bid me good evening and I nodded. I raised my hand, signaling them to stop. I wanted to see those children up close. We made small talk and I complemented them on their beautiful children. "You have a beautiful family", I said. With that, I bid them good-bye, turned from the top of the driveway and returned to the house. By the time I reached the porch I was once again greeted by a memory from the past.

THE SLAUGHTER HOUSE

One summer morning I received a telephone call from one of my classmates. Mike was the only black child in my class at St. Augustine Elementary school. He called asking if I would like to come to his house and spend the day. I was happy to hear from him as I had not seen him since school recessed for summer vacation. He lived a couple of miles from me so I rarely saw him during the summer break. He told me that his mother would drive to my home, pick me up and bring me home later that evening. I asked my mother if it would be all right and she said, "sure".

Mike lived on Moran Street, which was only a couple of blocks from where my grandmother lived, on Gallagher Street. I was thinking that possibly Mike and I might have the time to walk the few blocks to her home and visit with her. Grandma would be surprised and welcome us with arms wide open. Each time I visited her it seemed she always had something good for me. Mike and his mom showed up a few minutes later and we were on our way back to his house. When we arrived at his home, we went to his bedroom where he shared with me all of his toys and games. He had an aquarium in his room and on the wall was a dartboard. We spent a couple of hours playing various games and had a great time.

It was about lunchtime and Mrs. Tremain prepared some soup and sandwiches for us. I can almost here the old Campbell's Soup jingle, "Soup and Sandwich, Soup and Sandwich," do you remember it? One of Mike's best friends was also black; his name was Henry and lived next door. There was a knock on the door. "Hello, Henry," I heard Mrs. Tremain say. "Come in, have a seat, and join us for lunch." While we were eating, Mike's father had come through the door. He was a Detroit Police Officer and had stopped in for a bite to eat. He was a towering figure of a man with a light complexion and a soothing voice. We over-heard him talking to Mrs. Tremain about an investigation he was conducting in the neighborhood which concerned numerous incidents of vandalism associated with the Railroad crossing lights. It seems that vandals were breaking the lamps, which signaled on-coming traffic that a train was approaching. The location was at a point where the tracks crossed Conant Road. Mr. Tremain was convinced that a group of young boys living in the area was responsible for the damage. Mike and Henry knew most of the children in the area and were doubtful that any of their friends were suspect. The residents of the neighborhood were made up of about half white and half black, while the ethnic makeup of my neighborhood, a couple of mile away, was half Polish and half Italian.

While we were finishing our lunch Mr. Tremain asked us if we would like to do a little police work. We all said, "Yes". He thought that we might be able to identify the vandals if we saw them damaging the lights. At the end of Moran Street, a huge junkyard bordered the tracks. Moran St. was only a couple of blocks from Conant Rd. where the damages were occurring. His plan was to position us in the junkyard atop some crates looking over a high fence where we would have full view of the tracks. We went with him to the junkyard where he stopped briefly at the office and explained to the owner what he was doing. We then proceeded to a location along the fence, which ran parallel to the tracks. Mr. Tremain stacked some crates positioning them along the fence creating our surveillance station. He left us there and said he would return soon and that we must be vigilant, watching for any sign of trouble.

We had only been in our concealed position for a few minutes when we heard voices and noticed five teenage boys walking along the tracks. As they were approaching, we ducked down to stay out of sight. This group of boys was throwing rocks and cussing saying words and phrases, we had seldom heard before. Two of them were black and three were white. They had no perception of our presence or that their behavior was closely being scrutinized. Suddenly we heard the loud crashing of glass we witnessed one of the boys throwing a rock, destroying the red and green signal lamps that identified the rail switch. A moment later Mr. Tremain and another officer were hurriedly running down the tracks in an attempt to apprehend the boys. Three of the boys eluded capture but Mr. Tremain managed to take two of them into custody. He, with his captives, then proceeded to his scout car. He was lecturing the boys telling them that they were in significant trouble. As we sat, undetectable, behind the fence, we heard him say, "I want your names and the names of your accomplices and I want them now". He informed them that he has witnesses and that it was in their best interest to confess to their crime. He looked back at our location with a hearty thumb's up and then raised one finger indicating that he would be there shortly. When he arrived, he told us that the two boys had provided the names of the accomplices and that it would not be necessary for Mike, Henry and I to identify the individuals in the group. He expressed his thanks by handing each of us a silver dollar as he gave instructions to return to his home. As he departed for the police station, we paused for a moment waiting for the squad car to drive away preventing the two boys in the car from identifying us. We were pleased that we were of some help to the police department.

We left the junkyard saying good-bye to the owner. We returned to Mike's house via an alleyway. Mike and Henry were speaking of a nearby "Slaughterhouse" and wanted me to see it.

The slaughterhouse was a huge green building, which was set far off the road at the end of Moran Street. The building could not be seen from the street as it was concealed by a slope in the land that was covered by tall trees. The alley that we traversed ran directly behind the building. Approaching the location, we saw two raised truck-loading ramps. We stopped and watched the activities that were taking place. One ramp was used to unload livestock and the other was used to ship out the finished product. A line of windows at the top of the building covered the entire perimeter. There were a number of huge disposal trucks parked in an adjacent lot. Mike explained that all the waste from the animal processing was hauled away in them.

I can recall listening to the various sounds emitting through the perimeter windows. The cows and pigs seemed to be screaming. They somehow sensed that their end was near. About every 20 seconds, amid the screams, you would hear what sounded like a loud sizzle immediately followed by a bang. Henry said that the noise was from some sort of electrocution machine. Henry was knowledgeable of these things as his father was employed at the slaughterhouse.

I remember feeling poorly for the animals and told Mike and Henry that I had heard enough and that I would like to leave the area. We walked down the alley nearing the end of the building when we noticed a large open vat. A worker had just disposed something into it. We walked up to it and peered in to see what looked like ten or so little babies encased in clear membranes. Henry said," no that's not babies, that's unborn pigs", "there's always all kinds of unborn pigs in that vat"! Hey! Look! Some of them are still moving"! Watching them struggle and then die gave me a feeling of sorrow. I thought, "those unfortunate baby pigs". We returned to Mike's house a few minutes later telling his mother of all we had done and seen that day. It was time for me to return home and as Mrs. Tremain drove away, I waved farewell to Mike and Henry.

Mrs. Tremain spoke briefly to my mother expressing to her, as all mothers do, my many fine qualities and what a pleasure it was to have me there.

To this day, I have not been able to forget the sight of the infant animals in that disposal vat as they struggled and squirmed for life. The incident had a significant effect on me. The vision has recurred many times over the years.

It was about that time in my youth when Life Magazine had released an issue that featured a series of photos of unborn children still within the womb of the mother. These were remarkable photographs and represented a major breakthrough in this type of microphotography. I remember telling my mom that the pictures reminded me of the scene from the slaughterhouse. It was at that moment that I really began to realize the sacredness of human life and what a miracle it truly is.

Recalling my father's battle with death, I see my family and myself doing all that was humanly possible to extend his life. All of us hoped for a recovery and believed that he should be given every opportunity to rebound from his illness. He was with us for a few days longer. While he was lying in bed and in a semi-coma, I approached him and whispered my loving farewell into his ear. At that moment his eyes opened, he blinked and smiled. To me, he was saying, good-bye. His passing was peaceful and was a testament to the precious right to life we all have.

Even today, I aquatint the present day abortion houses and clinics with what I saw at the slaughterhouse. The laws, formed and shaped by man have reduced human life to that of farm animals to be disposed of at will or for a matter of convenience. The culture of the country at that time seemed to be transforming. Roe vs. Wade was just a few years away and an ominous outcome was forecast. Young women were told that, "It's alright, Do It! It's your right!" What a horrendous sin and crime. I, at that time, added another petition to my daily litany; please God, and humankind, "Save the Children". What lessons I learned that day.

It was now 6:00 PM.

I proceeded to walk outside to the rear of the house. Exiting the kitchen door and entering the garage, I stood still in the doorway leading outside. How many times in my life had I stood in this very spot? Standing there, motionless, Freckles came into my mind.

FRECKLES

Freckles was the name I had given to a stray cat that showed up one autumn day in 1999. During my difficult times, God has always delivered consolation to me. I viewed the arrival of this small creature in this way. I had no liking of cats. I think this stemmed from my youth when my neighbor presented me with a 4 week old kitten. I was five years old at the time. The kitten became very sick and I watched my mother try to nurse it to wellness by feeding it milk from an eyedropper. As it turned out, the poor thing had been weaned from it's mother a couple of weeks too soon. It died there in my mothers lap while I sat near her. I was overcome with grief and until the day that freckles arrived, I had no liking of cats.

Freckles came to me at a time when I needed a companion. She stood there, in front of me on that cool, late fall morning. I retrieved a saucer of milk for her as I felt she might be hungry. She lapped it up in an instant and we became friends. She came near to my feet and without notice jumped to my chest where she nuzzled into my warm jacket, purring and preening. I thought, what is this all about? I asked myself, why at this time have you arrived? Did God's angels send you to bring me peace? While I had my own struggles I was dealing with, Freckles brought me much solitude and friendship. She took up residence in the rafters of the garage and would greet me each morning as I entered the garage. Looking up I would see her and she would descend from the rafters and land gently on my shoulders seeking my touch atop her head. Petting her, she would look at my eyes beckoning me to provide her nourishment. I found that I looked forward to seeing her each morning.

For the next couple of months we became great friends and I cherished the connectivity I found in her. As abruptly as she had arrived, she was gone. It was mid winter, cold and snow blown. The rear garage door had been left open and freckles wandered off. With out letting on, I was filled with loss. She never returned that day and I could only hope that she strayed away only to find another in need of the comfort she could bring.

It was 6:15 PM. Still standing in the door way, looked up at the old basswood tree and recalled the following event.

THE LEAF THAT NEVER FELL

The winter of 2000 had arrived too early, just as my 52nd birthday had. The first snowfall came on October sixteenth and brought with is the regret that summer and fall had passed so quickly. For the past few years, we had been blessed with unusually mild winters and the fresh snow on the ground was a sure sign that when you live in Northern Lower Michigan you ought to count your blessings. Hopes for another mild winter were dashed that day. Celia said, "It looks like we're in for a long cold winter". I at once responded, "I believe we'll have another warm one, just wait and see." I knew she was right and my opposite opinion was more one of hope than fact. The past three winters were unusually mild due to a condition in the atmosphere known as El Nino. I had hoped that this Spanish named wonder worker would again wave his magic wand sending warm Southerly breezes to moderate the temperature in Michigan. Celia was exact in her prediction of what was to come.

The trees had shed most of their leaves by the end of September. Only a few remained attached and seemingly waited for the fateful breeze that would rip them from their stand. Before the end of October, we had been bombarded with a number of snowfalls that were allied with sleet, freezing rain and incredibly bone chilling winds. Only the barren skeletons of the trees and their branches remained as a stark silhouette against the gray background of the winter sky.

One morning as I walked outside to retrieve the newspaper I looked upwards and noticed one distinct leaf that had somehow been able to endure the wrath of this early winter weather. How astonishing, I thought. I had not noticed that leaf before. Where had it come from?

I concluded that somehow it had just been overlooked. As I looked upon the leaf, I could not help but wonder how it managed to cling to the branch, constantly being assailed by the elements. It had outlasted millions upon millions of leaves.

My mind began to conjure up all sorts of philosophical thoughts as I sought an explanation. The leaf was one of millions, yet it survived. This leaf, which was once part of an ornamental canopy, now stands out, splendid and proud, commanding recognition.

When the wind was calm the leaf would lazily relax as if to sleep. When the wind would gust, it immediately arose to attention like the raising of the flag seeking a salute. I speculated as to why I was witnessing this event. This moment of brief meditation was most calming but was quickly abandoned as it was nearing 7:00 am and I had to prepare to depart for work.

My thoughts drifted to the experience a number of times during that day. Looking outside, at the near blizzard conditions, I could not help but think that the leaf would surely have vanished by the time I returned home. After a somewhat treacherous journey home, I was relieved to find myself safely pulling into the garage, thankful but white knuckled. I opened the rear door of the garage and looked to the position of the leaf. To my astonishment, it still survived. The leaf was wildly flaying back and forth, from side to side and yet it somehow managed to defy nature clinging to its anchor. There seemed to be some elasticity to the stem and the branch to which it was attached. Once again, I found myself philosophizing and began to formulate a parable from the experience. I was convinced that the leaf would not fall, and somehow I knew it would defy all odds and in fact would accompany my meditations through the spring of 2001. Spring was still more than 3 months away.

A week or two had gone by and I decided to disclose these events with Celia. I told her about the leaf and led her outside to observe the object of my amazement. I wanted her to share in this happening that I found to be quite remarkable. I did not tell her that I felt I was receiving some sort of sign. She agreed that it was most unusual that this battered leaf somehow survived the elements.

The leaf was no longer just a leaf. In my mind, I looked upon this leaf as a delicate ornamental symbol. It served as an inanimate bridge to strengthen my faith. With three months of hard winter remaining, sub freezing temperatures, blizzard conditions and daily snowfalls, it was not likely that this icon would survive. It was now early December and the leaf still managed to hold fast. I was convinced that it resided there, on that branch, creating for me a daily moment of peace and serenity. Each morning without hesitation, I looked upward to be greeted by the sight of this banner, outwardly waving a friendly hello.

Christmas was fast approaching and the stresses of work and the season were particularly intense that year. Upon waking, I would gaze from the bedroom window to see how much snow that evening had brought. Each morning I would awake to find that two, four, six or more inches of new snowfall had fallen. Staying true to my daily ritual, I moved to the kitchen where I immediately prepared a pot of coffee. The rhythmic sound of the peculator signaled that it would not be long before I received my morning fix of caffeine. I began to wonder if the leaf would still be there when I went outside to retrieve the newspaper. Opening the rear door of the garage, I found myself looking ever so slowly upward to see if the leaf had withstood yet another day. These feelings persisted each day as my confidence slowly slipped, yet not entirely. Each morning I had the same thoughts; the leaf had surely been beaten down from its perch. With squinting eyes, I was reluctant to peer upward, half expecting to see this testimonial had been vanquished to the ground or nowhere in site. Although I found myself faltering, I was affirmed and for day after day the leaf remained.

In late December 2000, the county was pummeled with a number of severe storms. One particular blizzard dumped fifteen inches of snow, which was accompanied by thirty to sixty mile an hour gusts of wind. In complete amazement, I found that the leaf stayed vigilante over my morning invocation.

The weather in January and February was more relentless than that of November and December. Mother Nature had unleashed bitter cold and dreadful weather on the region and still, the leaf continued to exist. Against the dark contrast of the winter sky, the leaf stood out as the only visible sign of life as it defied all odds. The winter birds dared not venture out in this bitter cold, yet the leaf continued to wave and bid me good day each morning.

With spring still one month away, I was confident that this leaf would conquer the winter, and represent a victorious symbol of survival. There was no longer doubt or any lack of faith. I knew that the leaf would survive beyond March 21, the first day of spring. That first day of spring had come and gone.

I am refreshed at the recollection of this memory. I acknowledged an enhanced understanding of spiritual survival. This leaf, the object of this parable, became for me a symbol of life and the journey we all must make.

The leaf will never fall as it represents the resilience of the human spirit. The parable sends a message; "be not afraid". The relevance of this experience brings hope to the hopeless. It teaches us to be strong in faith, to resist adversity, and to celebrate life even in periods of trials and pain. Each of us clings to our own fragile branch of life. We weather the sunshine and the storms. When the bud of a leaf sprouted, wasn't it much the same as our own conception? When the leaf opened to its full splendor, wasn't that much like our life journey? As it aged and courageously fought the elements and somehow managed to cling to the branch, wasn't that, much like our own struggles to sustain ourselves? What influence have I had on the people I have met on my journey to this dream? What effect have I had on them?

This parable of the leaf helped me to make sense of my feelings. It helped me to understand my past and accept it as part of the journey I embarked on the day I was born. It reminds me of all I have done and all I have failed to do. Now as this first portal is about to open,

I realized that I was prepared for my journey by living the experiences of my youth. Those youthful experiences shaped my character and led me forward to adulthood. Like the leaf that held fast to its branch, I have tried to cling to the virtues that were nearest and dearest to my heart. Like the leaf, struggling.............never to fall.

As this story ended, my thoughts were greeted by the highlights of various delightful moments of the past. I viewed my wedding and the birth of my children. Countless scenes of happy moments filled with joy and laughter. I saw time and events encapsulated which encompassed the last 59 years. Scenes of Christmas mornings, birthdays and holidays came into view. I saw my children at all ages with their eyes filled with awe and wonderment. I heard the line from a song that said, "Let the children's laughter remind us of who we are." I had no recollection of bad times, for today, though it was going by fast, was a celebration. I looked at my watch; it was going on 7:00 PM.

I made my way to the old rocker, sat down and closed my eyes. In the next instant, I viewed what looked like an old newsreel from the fifty's. It was a kaleidoscope of portraits of remarkable people past and present, some real and some fictional. Each of them placed an indelible mark within my soul and mind. For a moment, each image came into view then faded to infinity. I saw Christ, St. Francis, Mother Theresa, Santa Claus, Al Kaline, Albert Einstein, Ben Franklin, George Washington, King Arthur, Father Flannigan, Robert Frost, Superman, Winston Churchill, Mike Ilitch, Robin Hood, Rev. Fulton Sheen, Roy Rogers, Davy Crockett, Raymond Bryan, Mom and Dad, Ivanhoe, Sir Lancelot, Don Quixote, Charles Tandy, Anne Frank, St. Bernadette, Andy Farkas, Dick Bagan, Paul Stockey, Lee Sullivan, Ralph Thorpe, Tarzan, Bill Taylor, Brucie Faener, Fr. MCCarthy, Aunts and Uncles, my children, grand children and great grand children, The Blessed Mother, Tony, and thousands more. I greeted each image with a nod and a smile as they passed my minds eye. I was able to recall biographical sketches of each of them. It was as if I had a personal relationship with each of them. I thought, how nice to recall all these souls who in someway had taken up space within my memory bank.

Knowing that I was being called I knew that those who had passed would be my welcoming committee. Time had no relevance for I was fully aware of my station sitting in the rocker. What fond memories, I thought. In the background, I could hear the sound of water cascading down a peaceful brook. The sounds came from a small, table top fountain I gave to Celia as a Christmas gift in 2002.

Gazing at it, and listening to the sound, I was reminded of rain. When I was a child, I viewed the rain as tears from heaven. I choose to believe that when it rains, the tears of all the Saints are cleansing us, providing Global Absolution. I stood and walked to the bay window. Today, there was no rain. I moved to the door and stepped upon the front porch. I raised my eyes to the sky, embellishing the beauty of this day. The Sun was slowly moving to the western sky signaling that the day was coming to and end.

Its rays cutting through the puffy clouds created a cascade of pastel colors, forming one of the greatest works of art I had ever seen. The hand of God painted this portrait. It was 8:00 PM.

Returning indoors, I found Celia in the kitchen preparing a meal. She was preparing meat lasagna, one of my very favorite dishes. It was rather late for dinner but time did not matter to me. This would be my last meal and I was pleased. I looked to my left and then noticed the portrait on the wall, which had hung there for 45 years. It was a lovely painting by, William Chadwick, entitled, "On The Porch". The painting is that of a woman, sitting stoically at a table. She appears to be in deep thought as she views all that happens around her. Many years ago, the painting inspired me to compose the following poem that I present here for you. The poem portrays the events that had taken place within the family over many years. It depicts these events as seen through the eyes of:

THE LADY ON THE WALL

The rooms' silent sanctuary

brings on meditation,

Thoughts reminiscing, a tear

makes a presentation.

The dimmed light...your solitude reveals,

Feelings of loneliness cannot be concealed.

A presence you sense..... a witness to it all,

Could it be.... the "Lady on the Wall".

Joys and sorrows, memories

of years past and gone,

Pictures and symbols, writing

the lyrics to a song.

These objects of moments,

they tend to remind,

An instant to re-live them

in your heart and mind.

Hearing a heart beat, and a distant call,

Could it be....the "Lady on the Wall".

The captivating scene,

presented to you graceful,

All you have seen,

yet you remain so peaceful.

Passion......Love......Anger......Pain,

All of God's virtues have been explained.

The lot you have witnessed

of human kind,

Stored so secretly somewhere in time.

From the place where you sit,

you'll never fall,

Could it be....."The Lady on the Wall".

Charm, dignity and peace

are the words you speak,

Looking upon your image,

you seem so meek.

The look of your eyes,

compassion and care,

Your love of life, the hat you wear,

A light breeze descends through the trees,

It carries a thought as well as the leaves,

Don't dwell on the things

that brings hearts to a stall,

Could it be...."The Lady on the Wall".

Promises made and promises broken,

Joyful times with gifts and tokens.

From toddlers to adults

the children have grown,

One, now two from the nest have flown.

Grandma, grandpas, and

grand children too,

Have often stopped to gaze at you.

From your tranquil seat

you appear to be small,

Could it be...."The Lady on the Wall".

Through the protective pane,

the passage of time,

Oh, silent observer,

you inspire this rhyme.

Of life's follies, you have kept a memoir,

Written in the stars, stored near, yet far.

You know the words spoken

and the words that were not,

You recall the tender moments

We may have forgot.

Hearing a heartbeat and a distant call,

Could it be...."The Lady on the Wall".

Holidays, anniversaries

and birthdays galore,

Sons, daughters and grandchildren more,

Brothers, sisters, uncles and aunts,

Playing music and singing,

a time for dance.

To life's emotions and passions

you haven't been blind,

Through tears and fears

You have stayed constant kind.

Never in anger, you look, down to see,

As the Sacred Hearts

Have been guiding thee.

Don't dwell on the things

that brings hearts to a stall,

Could it be....."The Lady on the Wall".

I meditated upon these words for a few moments and then my thoughts shifted to Celia. I wondered if she had discovered the anniversary message I had written her this morning. Returning to the bedroom, I looked to the top of the dresser and saw that the pages I had penned were no longer there. She had found my letter. I was drawn to the closet, where I looked to the top shelf and noticed a package that was wrapped in a white linen shroud. I reached for it and slowly removed the wrapping. It was a document I had written when I was fifty-four years old. It was my life as I had relived it this day. Upon stumbling across my writings, all had become clear. Somehow, I don't know how, I had written my own living eulogy. Word for word and event by event, this last day had followed every word I had written. I was unaware that my writings then would be prophetic and detail my last day on this Earth.

I went back to the kitchen; Celia greeted me with a tender smile for she knew what I had been looking for. With her apron attached and stained with sauce, she approached and embraced me whispering her hearts feelings. She said that what I had written gave her much happiness. I included prose and poetry I had written to her many years ago. Somehow, early this morning those words came back to me. She told me I had given her best gift ever. The moment was so tender. We sat down to a fine meal. I relished every bite. I told her that the lasagna was the best she had ever made. She smiled and said," You always say that". It was 9:00 PM.

The phone rang and I instinctively answered it. It was my son Ray. I said, "Hi Ray, how are you?" He said, "Dad, how did you know it was me?" I responded," I recognized your voice, saying jokingly; I have only known you for fifty-eight years. "Can I speak to mom? "Hold on", I replied. I sat there smiling as I heard her tell him of my extraordinary restoration. Celia asked him to call his brothers and sisters to let them know. He was instructed to tell them to call at once. Much of the next two hours was spent on the phone talking to each one of them. I received calls from my grand children as well. In between the call, I was greeted with hundreds of momentary glimpses of my past in full Technicolor. I saw vignettes of pitching coins against the Dairy Queen wall, hitting a home run in the playoff game, collecting and trading baseball cards, giving haircuts to my sons, Easter Sunday 1985, the beach at Empire. I saw the tree house I built, my wife's laughter, the sunset, vacations, walking on the beach in Hawaii, the sights of Hong Kong, the castles in France, the cruise on Lake Geneva.

It was 11:00 PM. Holding the hand of God, I hear, "your life here on Earth has been good and you have been greatly blessed." You have witnessed the culture of the world changing. You are being called but know that prayer will begin to return to public schools and institutions in 2011. Roe v. Wade will be overturned by 2012. Peace in the Middle East will arrive in 2016. Man will returned to the Moon in 2020. Many other revelations were disclosed……………………..

Blinking my tear filled eyes, I saw myself lying in bed. Celia was spoon feeding me broth and speaking non-stop. I noticed that I was unable to respond and had a distant look on my face. The calendar on the wall was for the year 2022 making me seventy-two years old at that time.

It was obvious to me, that this was the time that I had succumbed to Alzheimer's disease. It was clear that she had been caring for me for the past ten years for the actual year was 2032. During the revelation I learned of all the events I had missed. In this vision, I received 10 years of information about my children, grand children and great grand children. I learned of Celia's devotion, love and commitment. I felt her lips against mine, my eyes opened and the vision ended. I looked to the clock; it was 11:30 PM. I told her that it was time to rest.

I was tired and this special day, this life, was coming to and end. I changed into my pajamas, brushed my teeth and looked for her. I embraced her, closed my eyes, and kissed her with the passion of an eighteen year old. I told her that I had always loved her and that there never was any other for me. I told her that today I had a most wonderful experience. I mentioned to her that I knew in advance that this day was to come. I had been blessed and recovered memories of many of the joyful events of my life. I said to her, "The most joyful occasion in my life was the day we married". I thanked her for being there for me all these years and assured her that we would always be together. I cannot explain the happiness I felt at that moment. I asked her to bring the letter I had penned earlier that morning so that I could read it to her. I wanted her to hear my voice repeat these words with the passion that was intended. She went to her top dresser drawer retrieving the letter. With a slight tremble, she handed it to me. Looking into her eyes, I opened the envelope and unfolded the prose. It began, "My dearest companion, this journey we embarked on more than fifty-nine years ago has been more than words can describe. The blessing bestowed upon us are too numerous to list, yet they reside here in my heart. You have never failed us and for that, I love you more today than at the time of our meeting. I have loved you from the moment we met; it was truly, love at first sight. My love for you grows even now during the autumn of our lives.

Instinctively she tenderly caressed my left hand as I read on. Dearest, I have left you and our children a journal of my dream, this life. For the past twenty-eight years, it has been tucked away awaiting this day and this very moment. You will find it wrapped safely in the palm of my old Al Kaline mitt stored on the top shelf of the closet. I had written it years ago. I realized that with the onset of old age I was beginning to forget. This journal, this story, is a gift to you for everything that you have done and for everything, you are to me. No man that has ever lived could have been so fortunate as to find a person of your nature, your spirit and your heart.

I know that you have selflessly cared for me these past 10 years as I wandered aimlessly. You gracefully carried this burden, embraced me, and placed a kiss on my lips each day. This poem, written so many years ago, is yours. I have repeated it countless times.

A SONG FOR YOU

You, you came along,

Just when I needed you......

And I know, in my search for love,

I had found it, only in you.

When we first met,

My heart took flight, and

Has since, never come out of the clouds.

My mind had wandered...

And this imagination

Began the transformation, within me.

You, you came along,

Just when I needed you.....

And I know, in my search for truth,

I had found It, only in you.

Gazing to the sky,

When it is gray and dreary,

Among the clouds your eyes appear,

With the glow of the rising sun,

To imagine your face,

Your beautiful face,

Only made lovelier

By, the pleasure of your smile.

You, you came along,

Just when I needed you......

And I know, in my search for romance,

I found It, only in you.

My heart's journey has come true,

From the silence in my mind,

I hear the distant

Sound, that calls my name.

It lingers within,

Like a never-ending wish

For an endless, Daydream.

It repeats your name over and over again,

An endless love song

Called, Celia

You, you came along,

Just when I needed you,

And I know, in my search for faith,

I found It, only in you.

I have watched from afar,

Your lovely silhouette,

With the setting sun at your back,

Slowly, you stepped

Down, the sandy beach.

The sound of the serf,

The gulls and the leafs of the trees,

Seem to command your meditation.

For that moment,

A peaceful ascension

Takes hold of my being...

And my faith is restored

By God's gift, to me.

You, you came along,

Just when I needed you,

And I know, in my search for wonder,

I have Found it,only in you.

Joined in this journey,

Love has transcended life's trials.

When a tear drops,

When the sigh of heartache

Is yesterday's, memory,

When silence, gives way to understanding.

It is then that I bless you,

For, you are the flower of my life...

The stars in my world....

The magic in my mind.....

The passion in my eyes......

The kiss on my lips...

The love of my life....

The song in my heart....

You, you, have been here,

Whenever I needed you,

And I know, in my search for a song,

I have found it,

Only in a song For You

He signed it: Forever yours, Steve

I rose from the old couch and walked to the bedroom where I sat on the edge of the bed. I leaned back and laid my head on the pillow. The clock in the living room began to sound the Ave Maria as the chime bellowed 12:00 midnight.

Unafraid, I closed my eyes only to have them opened. Viewing the Light, my last thoughts.... I love you! Farewell! My spirit will be with you! See you soon! Tony extended his hand and led me forward. I entered this portal with one final thought, "Ask, and it shall be given you; Seek, and Ye shall find; Knock, and it shall be opened unto you". What He is speaking about is the doorway to Heaven. There is no mention of a key in this parable for it is understood that we, all of us, are not locked out unless it is by our own actions. The door can be opened to you, if you so choose. It is by our free will and understanding that this entrance awaits all of us.

Now, at the conclusion of this journey, I disclose this fact: It is simply this! These memoirs were penned when I was between forty-five and fifty-four years of age. I was compelled or should I say, inspired to document the course my life had taken. Certain things were revealed to me that I dared not ignore. I was constrained to create a literary time capsule that was not to be opened until the morning of my fifty-ninth wedding anniversary.

I recognized that at this time in my life, my ability to recall events was beginning to wane and the fear of Alzheimer's, this thief of the mind, would erase this history. Though one mans life means little to others, to me it meant everything. It is not for fame or fortune that I notate all these events but for the glory of the gift of life and the God given right to live it fully. When I completed this work, I carefully wrapped in a white linen shroud that Celia and I had acquired when we were in Malano, Italy, in 1987. Atop it, I placed a note that read, "Not to be opened until September 28, 2032." I concealed it in the palm of my old Al Kaline mitt and tucked it away on the top shelf of the closet. To this day it rests there. Grandma revealed that a separate note had been placed on the last page of the text. It read, "I will not be far from you. You shall discover two additional texts regarding this journey. They will have the titles of, "Half Way There: The Second

Portal", and "The Gate is Opened: The Final Portal". I asked Grandma if she had found them. She answered that she had and that in time she would reveal them.

Grandma then made the comment that everything he had written in, Journey to a Dream: The First Portal, had indeed come to pass. She stated that he had told her on more than one occasion that his last day would be the day of their fifty-ninth wedding anniversary. She recalled telling him that it was impossible for anyone to know the day or the hour of their passing, yet somehow he knew. She admitted that she had discovered the writings ten years earlier, during the period of his life when he had succumbed to the illness.

She told us that she was unable to contain herself and found it impossible to honor his wish that it not be read until the day of his death. Grandma had read the book many times and it was she that had placed it in the treasure chest. She told us that when the day had arrived he was resting peacefully upon his bed, going in and out of consciousness, unable to recognize her. Knowing that this day would be his last, she was resigned to end the journey the way that he had wanted it to end. She retrieved this chronicle from the chest and spent most of the day at his side reading aloud the entire text he had written. She, deliberately, stuck to the timetable of that day as he had written it, even to the point of preparing an omelet, soup and sandwich and meat lasagna. Through the course of the day, his demeanor and his appearance had changed. As she read the last line of the text; "Viewing the light, my last thoughts." I love you! Farewell! My spirit will be with you! See you soon!" She turned to see his face. His eyes then opened, gazing into hers' and a smile was delivered and one word spoken, "Celia". Caressing his hand and placing a kiss on his lips, his eyes closed and he breathed his last breath. She was convinced that his dream was fulfilled, just the way he had hoped.

Grandpa had included various poems and prayers he had written.

THE MESSAGE

A miracle had started within me,

and now outgoing is only love.

I have learned to be patient even when it is difficult and

now I listen intently

to the feelings, you wish to share.

I have forgiven all who have hurt me

and seek forgiveness in return.

My beliefs about the nature of life and people have been

wonderfully changed and I demand of myself to act

accordingly by searching for growth

in virtue and goodness.

Problems are now looked upon as new challenges for

which goals

are set to achieve them.

When you come to me with questions and concerns, I

hope you leave

feeling better and happier. To see kindness in your face,

your eyes and your smile will serve as an

evident expression of God.

Do not come to me in anger, or anger you may ignite.

Let us sit down and talk

with patience and understanding.

Keep your heart free from hate and anger. Keep your

mind free from worry

and be mindful of this daily.

Do not complain about adversity, push ahead to win

small victories

---they add up.

Remember that all prayers begin as a silent wonder

before they became words.

Be aware of the personal responsibility you must accept

for your

actions or in time they may

turn you into a coward.

Never fall victim to one of the world's greatest sins,

failure to deliver on love.

When you give more than you receive-----I will

guarantee you that in the

End you will receive more.

I ask you to share in this understanding and allow

yourself to be moved by the

Compelling inspiration of Christ.

A HUMBLE PRAYER

Dear Jesus, grant me the courage to go forward and
discover the real me. Draw me close to You so that I
may find peace in your gentle hands. Remove from
me all my shortcomings, which have been for so long
conditioned within me. As I discover who I really am,
guide me to be ever aware that You are at my side. It
was through Your benevolent kindness that all has been
revealed to me. Hold my hand as I walk this journey.
I ask that You look at me not as I am but with deep
faith in the man that I can be. This day I surrender my
problems and anxieties to You, for I know that You
forgive and love me. I pray that I may make amends for

any hurt I have caused. To You I offer up my suffering.

I kneel before you broken in spirit and sorrowful for

my actions, thoughts and deeds. Make me ever aware

of the conditioned behavior traits that I have lived with

most of my life. Grant me the grace to think before

I speak and to be completely truthful in what I say.

May I always be able to recognize the times when I

slip and that you will be there to catch me when I, fall.

Into Your hands I surrender my feelings of self-pity,

loneliness, being self-serving, having anxiety, guilt,

confusion, shame, self-centeredness, thoughtlessness,

the fear of rejection, insecurity, having false pride and

making myself a false victim. Lift me up so that I may

never ignore the physical and emotional needs of others.

Teach me to love myself as you love me. Grant me the

wisdom to understand my past and to discover the real

person within. Keep me humble in my thoughts.

I have You for my council. May all your faithful people

grow a deeper love and respect for one-another. I

humbly implore Our Blessed Lady to intercede with

You, her Son, on my behalf. Guide me and rescue me from my transgressions. Dear Jesus, help me daily to seek and find the virtues of Hope, Faith, Patience, Understanding, Fortitude, Knowledge, Love, Prudence, Trust and Wisdom. Fill my heart with the Gifts of the Holy Spirit.

ODE TO HUMILITY

Lord, make me mindful of:

Not what I could have been but

What I can be.

Not what I have said but

What I will say.

Not what I have done but

What I can do.

Not on what I feel but

What others feel.

Not what I want but

What others may need.

Not Who I have hurt but

Who, I can help.

Not What pain I have caused but

What peace I can bring.

Not for Who likes me but

For You, Jesus, Who loves me, most.

THEN GOD CAME IN

What have I done for these many years?

Now, that I see the traces of your tears.

Will my heart ever know your sweet love?

The answer will come from the spirit above.

As I was lamenting on the trails of my sin,

A knock on Faith's door,

Then God came in.

Your beautiful nature, your tender heart,

Some how I managed to tear them apart

Unaware of my past and the devil's plan,

I must have been walking with him, hand in hand.

My minds eye saw your fears from within,

A knock on Hope's door,

Then God came in.

I see that an angel is holding your hand,

Your head on his shoulder, footprints in the sand.

Lifting your eyes to Heaven's place,

He extended His Hand, His loving embrace.

Mending your gentle heart, the time to begin,

A knock on Love's door,

Then God came in.

Who knows why God has led us down this road!

Breaking, me to my knees to carry this load.

The hurt I have caused is deep inside,

I beg God that peace, go there to reside.

Seeking forgiveness, I cry to Him,

A knock on Humility's door,

Then God came in.

My dearest darling, my motive is true,

I'll spend the rest of my life making it up to you.

Open your arms to me once more,

To your Faith and Compassion, I humbly implore.

Please laugh with me, cry with me and forgive me dear,

A knock on Sincerity's door,

For God has come in.

THE RING

By inheritance the century

Old home had come to me.

Finding the staircase to

The forth floor crest,

I happened upon an old chest that rests,

Covered in cobwebs though not buried,

What treasures does it hold? I wondered.

What secrets hide inside? I pondered.

Wiping away the dust a name appeared,

The owner of the contents, this was clear.

The rusted latch, at my touch,

Fell to the ground,

The clatter, to my ear,

Made, a symphonic sound.

Attempting to raise the top,

The hinges begged for oil.

With my eyes curious,

The chest beckoned me to see.

Placed inside, a note read,

Sealed with a kiss, 1863.

Upon examination

I began to remove memories,

So solemnly placed with precision care,

A small metal tin, a lock of gold hair.

A crystal jar of the finest kind,

No hint of the dried perfume remains

Crumbled rose petals layered

in linen wrapped satchel.

The thorn covered stem found there,

Identifying the flower,

Long departed, the color had vanished.

The ash forming, a perfect silhouette.

A withered boutonniere

From a gala dance,

A telegram that called

Him up to advance.

The tarnished button

From the cuff of his coat,

The red sash still tied in its tote.

All placed in succession,

She recalls the procession.

The proclamation of their

Wedding was also there,

Though dotted with the

Stains from her tears.

Ever so slowly, unwrap the

Cloth, ever so slow.

With each, unravel,

The linen crumbled as if to snow.

Ten wraps down it began to take hold.

Then ten more, an oak

Wood box to behold.

Perfectly preserved looking

New and polished,

The name engraved entered

My mind a second time.

Unhurriedly I lifted the lid

To find her, gifts of devotion.

Letters written in the finest hand,

Expressions of his love.

Count 100 and more,

Soon I'll be at your door.

Beneath the prose lies a ring

Bound, in a velvet pouch.

A card inside said,

"With this ring…ending at a tare.

A final card did I find,

On the inside page was written

To save the best in memories

I have done my dear,

I will visit you often,

Day by day and year after year.

From this lofty height out

The window I looked,

I spied in the courtyard directly below,

The face of a man upon a stone,

Rose to greet, my eyes.

Quickly I raced down flight after flight.

Entering, I walked to the stone,

This is holy ground, upon which I walk,

His image, gazing upwards,

Each day greeted her with a smile.

Engraved, his name first followed by hers and a simple

Inscription

That said, "I thee wed".

Each day after his passing,

Their vows were spoken, to the end.

"Cherished memories, of best of friends".

GOD'S HEALING DECREE

When you search for guidance,

You needn't go far for it to be seen,

just look to Ephesians 6:13.

When times seem tough and evil arrives,

just look to Mark 11:23,24 and 25.

When you seek the Spirit,

To within you be alive,

just look to Isaiah 53:5.

When your heart is longing,

To find the gateway to heaven,

Just look to Peter 5:7.

When you begin to see Christ,

Whose image abides in all men,

Just look to Matthew 24:7,8,9 and 10.

When your arms are outstretched,

And for grace, you ask, more,

Just look to Luke 24:6 and 34.

When sorrow fills your heart,

And life's joys seem lean,

Just look to Corinthians 14:15.

When the burdens you bare,

Appear to be so great,

Just look to Phillipians 4:6,7 and 8.

When you're down on your knees,

And your spirit is poor,

Just look to 1 Peter 2:24.

When your eyes fill with tears,

And no answer is seen,

Just look to Collosians 3:15.

When all seems to have failed,

And the evil one appears to have won,

Just look to the Great, Psalm 91.

SINCERITY

Poets throughout time

Have sung their songs,

All these emotions carried

Within for so long.

One's innermost feelings of love,

Are always, witnessed by the Spirit above.

The verses about good and bad have led,

To the clouds in our eyes

From the tears shed.

The vows we spoke with

Our hearts at rest,

So long ago, still stand the test.

Poets throughout time

Have sung their songs,

They speak of love and forget the wrong.

One's mind can punish

And destroy the heart,

That stored so much love

Back, at the start.

The tender thoughts of

Knowing you belong,

Between us, He formed,

This bond so strong.

Poets throughout time

Have sung their praises,

The quest for sincerity,

Our hopes it raises.

Our fragile hearts can be

Squeezed and drained,

But with love, our faith still remains.

Let the flower of forgiveness

Be your constant friend,

Knowing that love and

Graces He will send.

For between two, hand in hand,

Walking together to fulfill,

His marvelous plan!

Endless love

When God Commands

I looked, cross the meadow, to see and behold,

A Dove, an Eagle and an Angel of Gold.

Their eyes, beckoning, follow and live.

We know, you have much more to give.

Walk with Us, We are Peace, Strength and Light,

We have come to you, to calm the night.

They turned and slowly moved

Through the arch in the pines,

So not to loose sight, I followed behind.

Moving the branches which blocked my eyes,

The outstretched hand, of the Angel, caused me to sigh.

Walk with Us, We are Peace, Strength and Light.

We have come to you, to calm this night.

Up a great hill they ascended, as if to glide,

Be not afraid, we'll not let you slide.

When I reached the top, no soul did I find,

Overcome with fear, it played tricks on my mind.

Walk with Us, We are Peace, Strength and Light,

We have come to you, to calm this night.

So fast, the clouds were passing above my head,

Could I be at Heaven's Gate, of which I had read!

The wonder of it all opened my eyes to see,

The Dove, Eagle and Angel were standing next to me.

Walk with Us, We are Peace, Strength and Light,

We have come to you, to calm this night.

Return from this height and renew your fight,

We have this plan, know that it is right.

At one the Dove flew up, in radiant flight,

The Eagle then followed with all it's might.

Walk with us, We are Peace, Strenght and Light,

We have come to you to calm this night.

The Angel of God remained for a time,

Holding my hand he gave me this rhyme.

The gift you have been given comes from God's hand.

With Peace, Strength and Light, He bestows this

command.

Go forth in truth, sincerity and justice,

Knowing that, you are in my service.

Walk with Us, We are Peace, Strength and Light,

We have come to you to calm this night.

ABOUT THE AUTHOR

Stephen J. McKolay

4437 Wyatt Rd.

Traverse City, Michigan

49684

Born: 12-26-1950

One of 15 Children

Married to Celia 32 years

Six Children

This book is from a collection of short stories, part fact, and part fiction.

Short Biography: Stephen J. McKolay

Stephen J. McKolay was born at St. Johns Hospital, Detroit Michigan, on December 26, 1950. He was the third of 15 children. He was educated, through the eighth grade at St. Augustine Catholic School. His family relocated to the Western Suburb of Westland Michigan, where he completed High School at John Glenn High. He then attended various community colleges. He earned credits from Henry Ford, Wayne County and Schoolcraft Community Colleges. Later he attended Eastern Michigan University. He did not pursue his degree in Business Administration, though he earned 138 Credit Hours.

During this period he way employed by Mike Ilitich, owner of Little Caesars Pizza. Little Caesars Pizza at this time had 10 locations. As Little Caesars began to expand its operations, he traveled throughout the Mid-west and Canada assisting in the opening many locations. In 1973, upon leaving Little Caesars he sought employment with Radio Shack, then Tandy Corporation. Radio Shack Corporation has employed him to this day, 34 plus years.

In that same year he married Celia Bryan, his wife if 34 years. They resided in Westland, Michigan, for the first seven years of their marriage. Together they have six children and since 1980, they have resided in Traverse City, Michigan, where he has managed that Radio Shack location. His career with Radio Shack has been very eventful, allowing him and his wife to travel to many places in the world because of sales promotions and contests. He presently is the all time sales leader within the company, boasting over 10 Million dollars in personal sales.

He always has enjoyed writing and especially began to take it more seriously while attending the Eastern Michigan University where his instructor encouraged him to continue writing. With his many responsibilities at home and work, the pursuit of writing was random at best. Writing became recreational and only a dream of the future.

From his memories, he recalls observations and events experiences that he incorporates into this, his first completed book of a continuing trilogy, Journey to a Dream: The First Portal.

In 2007, he will reach his 57th birthday. He to this day embraces the virtues of love, loyalty and commitment, in all aspects of his life. He has lived his life by following a precept installed in him by his father when he was a youth. That precept was simply this; Order your life, with regard to daily conduct, by placing God first, followed by your family, country and employer, in that order. With respect to others, strive to show kindness in everyday life to all you meet whether it is school, work, social or political involvement.

Printed in the United States
126021LV00001B/56/P